IDeas For carDmakers

WITHDRAWN
FROM
STOCK

SEARCH PRESS

IDeas FOR CarDMakers

Over 50 TEMPLATES AND HUNDreDS OF Variations

Fransie Snyman

6433982

First published in paperback
in Great Britain 2016
Search Press Limited
Wellwood, North Farm Road,
Tunbridge Wells, Kent, TN2 3DR

Originally published in South Africa
by Metz Press
1 Cameronians Avenue
Welgemoed, 7530 South Africa

Copyright © Metz Press 2016
Text copyright © Fransie Snyman
Photographs copyright © Metz Press

PUBLISHER
Wilsia Metz

DESIGNER
Liezl Maree

PHOTOGRAPHER
Kenneth Irvine

TRANSLATOR
Amanda Taljaard

PROOFREADER
Susie Dinneen

REPRODUCTION
Color/Fuzion, Green Point

PRINTED AND BOUND BY
TWP Sdn. Bhd., Malaysia

ISBN 978-1-78221-441-0

CONTENTS

Introduction

Very few things are treasured as much as a handmade card. Cardmaking has dual benefits – firstly, it has therapeutic value for the creator; and secondly, it delights the recipient. The greatest gift you can give someone is time – some of your time. When you create a card with care for someone special, you give a little of yourself.

Creating cards should be fun for any keen crafter, but sometimes it is difficult to get started. You may fear that your design will not be striking enough, or perhaps you are facing so many options when it comes to paper, cardstock and embellishments that you are too overwhelmed to knuckle down to the task. I have also spent hours thinking about a card – too careful to start pasting for fear that it may look dreadful or that I will waste my stunning paper.

Each card that you make is an expression of your creativity; so there is no right or wrong way to go about making one. However, having a good plan at the outset is invaluable, and that is the purpose of this book. You will be amazed to discover how quickly you can make a card – often faster than shopping for one!

Card templates may well become your secret weapon. They can save lots of time and help you when your creativity temporarily leaves you in the lurch. When you set off with a good, basic plan, you can make any card very quickly – which will come in handy if the party starts in an hour's time and you stdon't have a card yet.

A card template is a layout and blueprint devised beforehand, and you can use it creatively by incorporating your own ideas. When you follow a template, it is easy to determine exactly what you will need, and the project can be completed easily, because all the important decisions have been made for you. You do not have to follow the templates exactly, but it serves as a good point of departure and stimulates your creativity.

The styles and techniques involved in card crafting are constantly changing, and while I love simple cards, others prefer interesting detail and adornment. Because so many people helped me to make these cards, the ideas in this book are sure to appeal to a wide audience.

If you do not have the specific colours or finishes used for the cards in this book, be inspired to use what you have. You may be familiar with other techniques that could be used to make a specific card – by all means, use them.

Since most of the cards were made using products that I bought over the years, no product specifications have been provided. The idea is really that you use your own paper and embellishments.

Hints on how to use the templates

Each template can be adapted in various ways to meet your requirements. You can rotate the template, flip it and even reduce it to make smaller cards. The possibilities are endless – especially when you combine more than one template and allow your imagination to lead the way. If you deviate from the template completely, that is fine too – perhaps a specific design simply inspires you to start making a particular card.

The templates can be used exactly as they have been printed or you can rotate them clockwise or anticlockwise, invert them, flip them or use a combination of these. Also feel free to add or omit elements. The template is just a point of departure so you can play to your heart's content.

Supplies

There are certain supplies which crafters, and especially cardmakers, simply cannot do without. Each example has a list of the supplies needed for that specific project. Make sure that everything is ready before you start, thus preventing a frustrating supply search once you are halfway.

Basic supplies

CUTTING IMPLEMENTS AND MAT

A good craft knife, scissors, and guillotine are the most basic implements required for cardmaking.

If you use a ruler while cutting with a craft knife, it is advisable to use a metal ruler. A plastic ruler is less sturdy and you may damage it with your craft knife. You can use special scissors for decorative edges on your cards, as well as dedicated cutters for perfect rounds, ovals and other shapes.

When using felt or fabric for your cards a dedicated pair of scissors is essential. Few things are more frustrating than having to cut felt with blunt scissors. If you decide to tear you paper for effect, control the tear by means of a special tearing ruler.

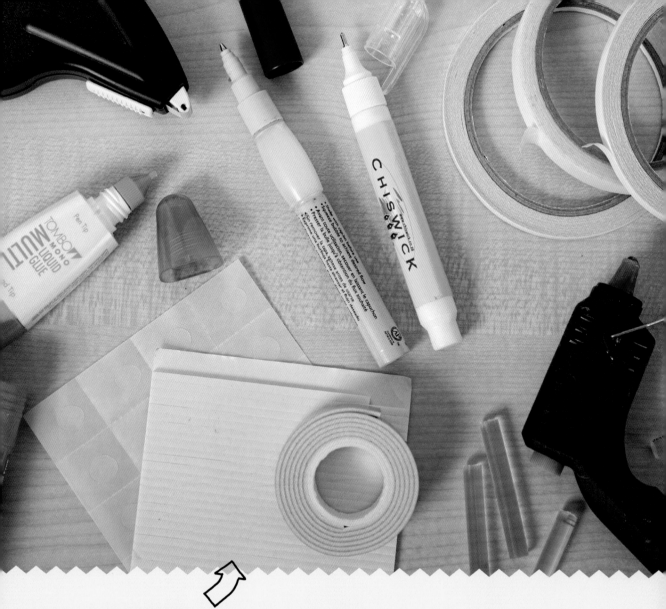

GLUE AND OTHER ADHESIVES

If you use the wrong glue for your project, you could ruin the appearance of the card completely. Most crafters have specific preferences when it comes to the type of adhesives they like to use. I have used the following:

☆ A glue pen – for very delicate pasting.
☆ Double-sided tape – to stick ribbon to card, as well as to join large pieces of paper and card. It is available in various widths. I prefer to use the narrowest tape bdecause if one accidentally pastes it askew, it can be removed more easily than a broader strip. To attach larger areas, I simply use more than one strip.

☆ Glue wheel – to stick smaller pieces of paper and card together. It can be used instead of double-sided tape, but it is not equally adhesive.
☆ Glue dots – to fix trimmings to cards. Glue dots are available in various sizes and stick firmly to most surfaces.
☆ Adhesive foam tape or foam squares – to add dimension to cards. When you use it, the pasted object is elevated slightly.
☆ Masking tape – to attach certain parts temporarily, for example for iris folding or when you are doing embossing work on a light box.

CRAFT PUNCHES

The variety of craft punches available today is amazing – I have a whole suitcase full of punches and I would love to have even more! The beauty of using punches is that one can create truly wonderful cards with little effort, using little paper. I am sure many card makers share this view. Even when using basic shapes, like squares, circles and hearts, you can create interesting pictures. To ensure that your punches serve you well, you must look after them and store them neatly. Manufacturers suggest different ways of sharpening punches. Some suggest that you punch through layers of wax paper, while others say that you should punch through a few layers of aluminium foil. You should experiment to find what works for you. However, if you do not regularly use the punch on thick paper, it should remain sharp for some time.

MATERIALS FOR STAMP WORK

Some of the projects in this book involve stamp work. Stamp work was especially popular when handmade cards came back into fashion. The stamps that were available then were mainly rubber ones mounted on wood. These are still popular and a large variety is available. Transparent stamps mounted on acrylic are easier to use, because you can see exactly where your design will appear.

Stamping requires inkpads, and they are available in a vast variety of colours and types. After you have stamped a design on a card, you can sprinkle it with embossing powder to provide a neat finish. A heat gun is used to set the embossing powder.

INK, GLASS PAINT, AND GLASS PAINT PENS

Alcohol ink is used to create the most exquisite backgrounds on glossy paper and non-porous surfaces. A special applicator is used to apply the paint. Glass paint does not necessarily have to be used on glass. It also works well on acetate (transparencies) and thick, clear plastic. The glass paint pens or markers that are available nowadays make it so much easier to work on glass and acetate – especially if you need to cover small areas. These pens are used in a few of the examples in this book.

STICKERS

Stickers are great embellishments for cards, and are very easy to use! They range from really plain to small works of art. If you use a sticker that is a work of art in itself, you may find that you do not need any other trimmings.

PAPER AND CARDSTOCK

Paper and cardstock are available in various sizes and thicknesses. The weight of the paper is an indication of its thickness. Paper of 80 gsm (grams per square metre) is suitable for everyday use and printing. Tissue paper can weigh as little as 15 gsm. Paper that is suitable for the making of cards varies between 160 and 250 gsm. I prefer working with paper that weighs 230 gsm because it is not too thick and it folds easily. Paper that is thicker than 250 gsm is regarded as cardstock.

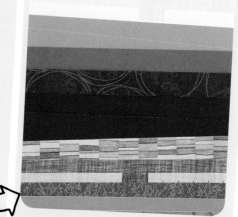

Shops that stock scrapbook paper are inexhaustible sources of decorative paper. Because of the variety available today, you will hardly need anything more for your cardmaking projects. Ordinary patterned paper is also readily available at craft shops and any shop that stocks paper.

Handmade paper is also extremely popular among card makers; even just a dash of handmade paper can make a card look stunning.

Paper is available in a number of sizes, such as A1 (60 × 84 cm) (23½ × 33 in), A2 (42 × 60 cm) (16½ × 23½ in), A3 (42 × 30 cm) (16½ × 11¾ in) and A4 (30 × 21 cm) (11¾ × 8¼ in). I have also made extensive use of scrapbook paper, which usually measures approximately 30.5 x 30.5 cm (12 × 12 in).

EMBELLISHMENTS

An assortment of embellishments is available to use on cards. Metal embellishments (charms), paper flowers, ribbon, handmade stickers, beads, split pens, buttons, and sequins can be used to add finishing touches to your work.

Self-adhesive rhinestones and pearls are very handy and are sometimes all you need to turn a boring card into something extraordinary.

WASHI TAPE

Washi tape is very popular and you will note that it is frequently used to decorate the cards in this book. It is extremely versatile and can be used for a considerable number of projects.

Washi tape is paper tape that was first made in Japan, but today it is produced worldwide. It is made from fibres from the bark of a specific tree, and is completely biodegradable. It resembles masking tape.

It is easy to use and, because it is initially not sticky, it can easily be peeled off should you accidentally paste it imperfectly. When you are entirely satisfied with the result, you can rub over the tape firmly and rest assured that it will not come off easily. The longer it remains on an object, the more difficult it is to pull it off.

RIBBON, STRING AND CORD

The various widths and colours available can add those beautiful final touches to cards.

Other implements that are not really necessary but which can really make your life so much easier include:

- ☆ Bone folder – to make indents and perfect folds in paper. It can also be used to smooth paper to ensure that adhesives stick firmly.
- ☆ Embossing pen – a blunt-nosed tool, the points of which are two different sizes, used for embossing paper and metal.
- ☆ Heat-gun – used with embossing powder for embossing of cards. It can also be used for general heating and melting.
- ☆ Teflon craft mat – it has a Teflon coating and can really simplify your life. This specific mat protects your work surface against stains, glue, and heat. Nothing sticks to this mat.

- ☆ Scoring tool – this tool is one of the best investments I have made. It is fairly easy to obtain but, unfortunately, usually marked in inches. When I came across one marked in centimetres, I bought it immediately.

Terminology and techniques

This is an explanation of some terms and techniques that are relevant to most cards.

CUT, SCORE AND FOLD

It is certainly easier to buy pre-cut cards, but then you are limited to what is available in shops. I usually buy larger pieces of cardstock and paper and cut them to the required sizes myself. Poor and skew cutting is quite conspicuous, and if you notice that something has not been cut neatly, others will notice it too. So make absolutely sure that your knife, scissors, and guillotine are razor sharp ensure straight, clean edges. When you have finished cutting the card, you can score it using a bone folder. It is easy to score a straight fold line when you are working on a cutting mat on which measurements are indicated. If your mat does not have measurements, you can indicate the fold line lightly in pencil. Score the line using a scoring tool, fold the paper along the scored line, and crease the fold, again using the scoring tool.

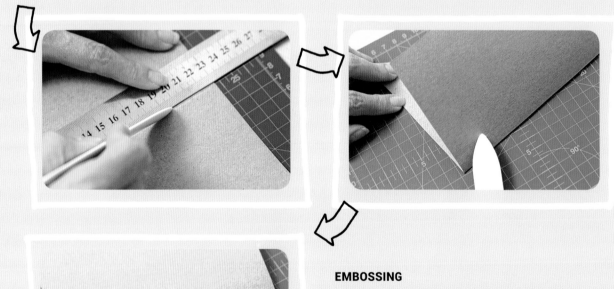

EMBOSSING

Motifs that are stamped onto cards appear more beautifully finished if you use embossing powder. Press the stamp onto the cardstock and sprinkle embossing powder over the print. Heat carefully, using a heat-gun, to melt the powder. Ensure that the ink is still wet when you sprinkle the powder over the motif and be careful not to burn the paper with the heat-gun.

IRIS FOLDING AND TEABAG FOLDING

Iris and teabag folding techniques have been used for some of the cards. My previous book is a good source of information on these and other techniques.

ATTACHING RIBBON TO CARDS

It is sometimes difficult to prevent the glue from showing through or spreading around the ribbon when you are attaching ribbon to cards. This can ruin the card. The easiest way to attach ribbon is to use the narrowest double-sided tape. This allows you to remove the ribbon easily should it need straightening. It is easier to fix the double-sided tape to the paper first and then smooth the ribbon onto it.

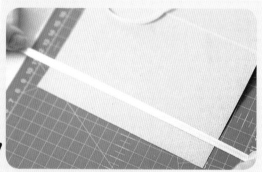

MATTING

When you paste cardstock or paper of various sizes on top of each other or layer them, it is called matting. Matting adds dimension to your design and can also be used to emphasise certain aspects. Cut the consecutive layers so that the edges differ by approximately 5 mm (¼ in). To add more dimension to your matting, use foam tape between the layers.

Design principles

There is a difference between the elements of design and design principles. Elements of design include aspects such as line, form, direction, shape and size, texture, colour and value. Design principles refer to: balance, repetition, focus, and harmony. Since this is not an academic book, I am not going to discuss each of these principles and elements in detail; instead, I shall focus only on those relevant to cardmaking.

FOCAL POINT

The focal point is one of the most important principles of design and, fortunately, it is also the easiest one to master. It is important that every work of art, be it a card, painting or sculpture, has a point of focus. This is the part which immediately catches the eye. The stronger the focal point, the better the ultimate design of your card will be. It is, therefore, worth your while to spend a few minutes contemplating the focal point.

The point of focus can be created by using colour, contrast, and shape. It can be positioned in the centre of a card or more to one side. It is usually the largest or brightest element on the card, but it may also be comprised of a few smaller elements that are grouped together. If you use more than one element to create the focal point, it is always better to use an uneven number, for example three or five instead of two or four. Group the elements closely together, or allow them to overlap to form one cluster. The smaller elements do not necessarily have to be the same.

REPETITION

Repetition is an important design principle and is especially striking if executed effectively. Repetition without variation can be dull and monotonous. A subtle change in the pattern that is repeated ensures variety and appeal.

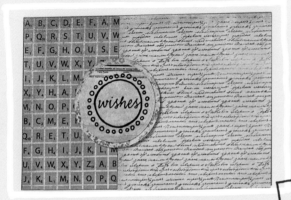

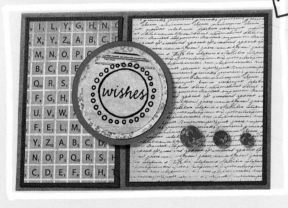

TEXTURE AND DIMENSION

Various items can be used to provide texture and dimension. You can use different layers of paper or embellishments, or assorted adhesives, for example large glue dots or foam types of varying widths.

The example on the left illustrates how the appearance of a card can be improved by simply adding a little texture and dimension.

HARMONY

Harmony is difficult to explain; essentially, it refers to the overall impression created by a card. You have to make sure that all the elements on the card match well. No sections should jump out or bother you.

THE TEMPLATES

Square 1

Card: 14 x 28 cm (5½ x 11 in) – fold into a square
A: 3 x 3 cm (1¼ x 1¼ in)
Distance from all the edges: 1½ cm (½in)

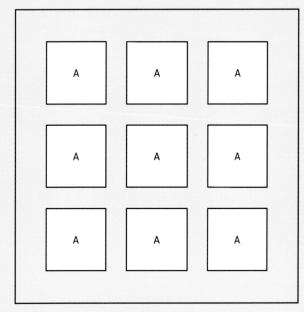

These templates are for cards measuring 14 x 14 cm (5½ x 5½ in), but you can adapt the measurements to suit your needs. The sizes of the various components used on the cards can also be adapted, depending on the paper and embellishments that you choose. Should you wish to use other shapes on the card, feel free to do so.

■□□□ FESTIVE CHRISTMAS

The squares on the Christmas card are pasted diagonally. Pewter squares with green metallic Christmas trees create a festive feel. The words in the centre are printed on washi tape and pasted onto dark-grey, glossy paper. The red buttons in the top corners and in the bottom centre are crystal stickers pasted onto bits of washi tape, then cut out and pasted onto the squares.

□■□□ LOVE IS IN THE AIR

The squares on this card are cut out and patterned paper is pasted onto the reverse side. It is then decorated with a heart sticker and one that resembles a diamond ring. Flowers in opposite corners and glitter glue along the edges of the squares complete the card beautifully.

□□■□ MOTLEY MIX

A jolly, brightly coloured card that is perfect for a child. The square in the top right-hand corner is deliberately pasted askew to emphasise the little robot. The finishing touch is a piece of bright red cord.

□□□■ CHIC SQUARES

Lots of matting is used on this classic, chic card. The nine squares are constructed by layering three pieces of paper. Each layer is attached to the previous one using foam tape to add dimension. Glittery gold paper is used for the first layer, followed by matt black paper and, finally, patterned paper. Each consecutive layer is 0.2 cm (⅛ in) smaller.

Square 2

Card: 14 x 28 cm (5½ x 11 in) – fold into a square
A: 7 x 6.5 cm (2¾ x 2½ in)
B: 8 x 7.5 cm (3¼ x 3 in)
C: 6 x 6 cm (2¼ x 2¼ in)
D: 6.5 x 4 cm (2½ x 1½ in)

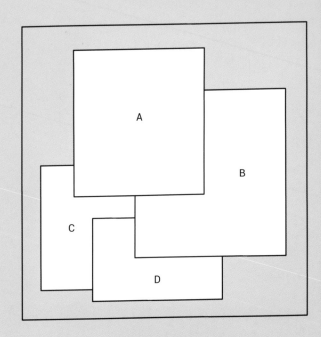

■□□□ NUMBERS

The template has been adapted by using three blocks of patterned paper on a patterned background. This works well despite the different patterns on the paper. The matted background and the block of white paper bring together the different elements.

□■□□ STYLISH HEART

The repetition of the pink paper and the patterned paper makes this a truly striking card. The big heart in the left-hand corner provides a lovely finish. Red glitter glue is used to define the squares beautifully.

□□■□ TURQUOISE WATCH

The black and turquoise work really well together on this card. The black motifs are laser-printed onto acetate, and pasted onto a turquoise background. The turquoise and black matting provides a stunning finish.

□□□■ WORDS OF LOVE

Using red and black together creates a stiking card. The words add interest and meaning while the black square in the corner holds all the lements together.

Square 3

Card: 14 x 28 cm (5½ x 11 in) – fold into a square
A: 12 x 12 cm (4¾ x 4¾ in)
B: 10 x 10 cm (4 x 4 in)
C: 8 x 8 cm (3¼ x 3¼ in)
D: 4 x 4 cm (1½ x 1½ in)
E: circles, 2 cm (¾ in) in diameter

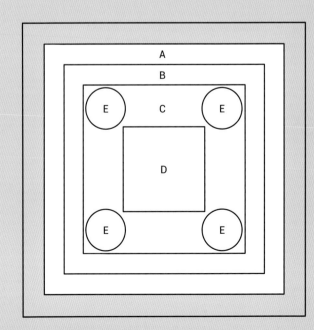

■□□□ RETRO DREAMER

The patterned paper helps to bring together all the components. The second square is outlined with strips of floral washi tape. The sides of the bottom square are also decorated with washi tape. The sticker that is pasted onto foam tape in the corner gives the finishing touch to the card. Because of the size of the sticker, the other corners need no embellishments.

□■□□ ON THE ROAD AGAIN

The card is slightly larger than the template, measuring 15 x 15 cm (6 x 6 in). The outside edges are decorated with washi tape. A black square with a smaller, red-and-black chequered-paper square is used in the centre. An extra brown triangle is added, and so is a little wooden car. The components used in the corners complete the card beautifully.

□□■□ DRAMATIC HEART

The variety of paper and the matting technique make this card truly unique. An extra white frame in the centre emphasises the vivid black-and-white heart. The four small, red hearts in the corners add the finishing touches and highlight the large red heart of the centre motif.

□□□■ FORMULA 1

This is a lovely card for boys of all ages. The black-and-white square onto which the yellow square and the little car are pasted, highlight the theme of this card. The black beads in the corners of the yellow square and the red glitter glue touches on the black-and-white square provide the ideal finish for this cute card.

Square 4

Card: 14 x 28 cm (5½ x 11 in) – fold into a square

A: 12 x 12 cm (4¾ x 4¾ in)

B: 14 x 2.5 cm (5½ x 1 in)

C: 6.5 x 4.5 cm (2½ x 1¾ in)

D: circle, 4.5 cm (1¾ in) in diameter

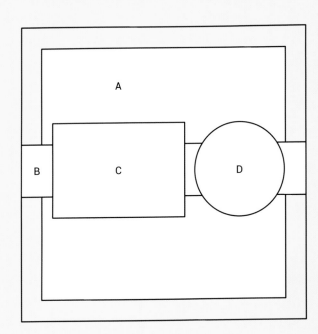

METALLIC HEART AND FLOWER
■□□□

The template is adapted slightly as an extra rectangle and heart have been added. The heart is punched from foil that has been embossed using a Cuttlebug™. To highlight the heart, it is pasted onto a dark-grey rectangle that has also been embossed using the Cuttlebug™. The big orange flower used instead of a circle provides a beautiful finish.

BIRDIE IN A TREE
□■□□

The paper has been cleverly used to follow this template. The tree and birdie motif on the paper is cut out and used with the shapes. This card is a perfect example of how you can tap into your creativity to adjust the layout so that the selected paper really stands out.

LOVE
□□■□

The combination of black and green works beautifully on this card. The rectangular section consists of three strips of washi tape, each pasted immediately below the previous one, on the green paper. The big red-and-black flower in the place of the circle is striking, and the three little red circles along the left-hand side put the finishing touches on the card. The wooden word combines the elements beautifully.

BEST WISHES
□□□■

This card is a perfect example of how the layout of a template can be changed. The combination of earthy colours lends a classic feel while the white background, together with the wording, makes this card really exceptional. The green-and-white matting on the rectangle provides a stunning finish.

Square 5

Card: 14 x 28 cm (5½ x 11 in) – fold into a square
A: 12 x 3 cm (4¾ x 1¼ in)
B: 10 x 3 cm (4 x 1¼ in)
C: 8 x 3 cm (3¼ x 1¼ in)
D: oval, 10 x 4.5 cm (4 x 1¾ in)

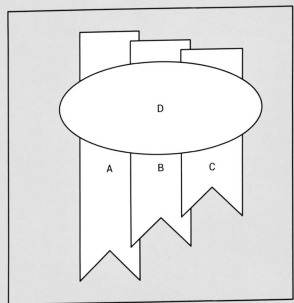

■□□□ EASTER

The oval on this card is slightly bigger than indicated. The matting technique used on the oval makes it a fabulous focal point. The ribbon matches the paper perfectly and stands out because the strips do not overlap, as illustrated on the template.

□■□□ STYLISH ROSE

The oval here is smaller than the one on the template, and the extra rectangle pasted under the oval works really well. The colour scheme is quite remarkable, and the various patterns on the three strips of ribbon add an interesting touch. The focal point is definitely the fabric autumn leaf and the heart made of tiny entwined twigs.

□□■□ TEABAG FAN

A great deal of washi tape is used for this card. A strip of pink-and-white washi tape is pasted along the top and bottom edges, as well as along the left edge. The oval is replaced by a circle of pink and white matted paper. A fan, made according to the teabag-folding technique in my previous book, is pasted inside the circle. A button forms the centre of the fan. Washi tape is used for the three ribbons on the right. Since the ribbons are wider than the tape strips, the tape is first pasted onto white paper (two strips, one below the other) and then cut.

□□□■ BLACK AND WHITE

A black-and-white arrangement always looks stylish and striking. The oval is again slightly wider and shorter than indicated on the template. The edges of the card are finished with black-and-white washi tape, and strips of fabric ribbon are arranged under the oval. The oval is highlighted by the matting technique and the fact that the white section has been embossed using a Cuttlebug™.

Square 6

Card: 14 x 28 cm (5½ x 11 in) – fold into a square
A: 10.5 x 3 cm (4¼ x 1¼ in)
B: 10.5 x 4 cm (4¼ x 1½ in)
C: 12 x 1.5 cm (4¾ x ½ in)

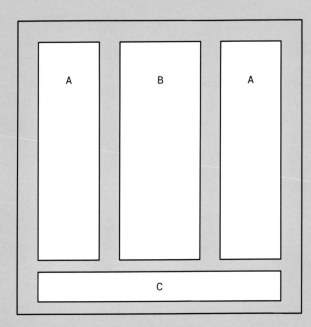

A	B	A

C

■□□□ CHRISTMAS SIMPLICITY

This design is very simple, and the success of the cards made according to this template depends solely on the paper and embellishments used. What makes this plain, silver card so striking is the stunning paper. The text along the bottom edge is printed on washi tape ribbon.

□■□□ PEARLY FINISH

The paper used for the rectangles matches beautifully. It is mounted on light-cream cardstock and the edges are chalked. The adhesive pearls add the final touch.

□□■□ WIRE FLOWERS

The flowers made of wire really suit this card. The message forms the lower rectangle, and the silver-and-white matting matches the wire flowers marvellously. The crisp green of the cardstock looks lovely with the silver and white.

□□□■ DELICATE ROSES

Because the paper used for this card is gorgeous, it works perfectly for this simple design. The matting technique in dark and light pink emphasises the stunning paper. The circle with the fabric flower in the left-hand corner creates an interesting focal point.

Square 7

Card: 14 x 28 cm (5½ x 11 in) – fold into a square
A: 12 x 8.5 cm (4¾ x 3⅜ in)
B: 8 x 8 cm (3¼ x 3¼ in)
C: 6 x 6 cm (2¼ x 2¼ in)
D: 12 x 2.5 cm (4¾ x 1 in)

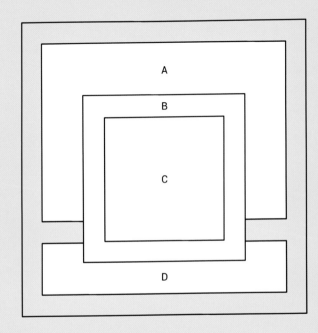

■☐☐☐ PINK WITH SILVER

The black flower in the corner of the inner square is an interesting addition to this design. The motifs of the patterned paper used here complement each other beautifully. The heart-lined edge is punched and it gives the card a charming finish. This card is slightly bigger than the template, measuring 15 x 15 cm (6 x 6 in).

☐■☐☐ DOTTY PINK

Exciting pink frames with little white dots make this an interesting card. The circle in the left-hand corner has been added to the design. The other corners are shaped with a corner punch to soften their appearance. The patterned paper is alternated beautifully with plain pink paper. You can add a message to the white square in the centre.

☐☐■☐ SWEET AND SIMPLE

The edges of the patterned paper in the top rectangle are chalked to add definition. The little flower in the left corner of the squares, and the organza ribbon, add the finishing touches.

☐☐☐■ DAINTY PINK ROSES

The centre square is moved a bit to the right. The little roses on it provide a beautiful finish. The patterned paper is really exceptional and that is what makes this card so striking. The tiny pink bow adds the final touch.

Square 8

Card: 14 x 28 cm (5½ x 11 in) – fold into a square
A: 19 x 4 cm (7½ x 1½ in) – trim the corners
B: 2 circles, 3 cm (1¼ in) in diameter
C: oval, 10 x 6 cm (4 x 2¼ in)

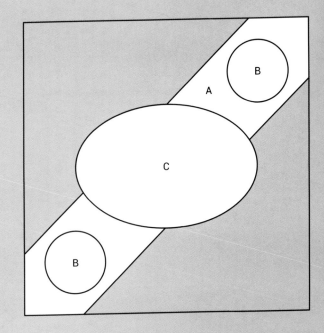

■□□□ STYLISH OVAL

Washi tape is used for the diagonal ribbon. A triangle of black-and-silver glitter paper is pasted above the ribbon, and a dark-green triangle below it. The lovely black-and-white oval frame is highlighted by matt black and green glossy paper. The little white flowers on either side of the oval emphasise the frame, while the three tiny flowers in the corner provide a charming finish.

□■□□ A DASH OF COLOUR

Both sides of the wide white ribbon in the centre of the card are finished with a narrow strip of grey washi tape. A wider tape strip is pasted onto the middle of the ribbon. The oval and circles are cut from the same patterned paper and finished using the matting technique. A red flower gives the centre oval a dash of colour and, together with the black and white flowers, completes the card beautifully. The little black flowers are pasted onto the circles to add the finishing touch.

□□■□ BUTTON FINISH

The oval on this card is made of an old coaster that is coloured with a milky pen, and the edges are chalked. The diagonal ribbon is made up of four washi tape strips; the centre strips are mirror images. This cute card is finished with orange paper circles, onto which a white and then a smaller turquoise button are pasted.

□□□■ BURGUNDY AND GREEN

The interesting combination of colours makes this a striking card. The wide, diagonal, grey strip is jazzed up using washi tape with a bright floral motif. The matting technique and a pretty little flower are used to highlight the oval. The same colours are used for the matting of the circles, and the tiny flowers with their self-adhesive rhinestones add a lovely finishing touch.

Square 9

Card: 14 x 28 cm (5½ x 11 in) – fold into a square
A: 14 x 6.5 cm (5½ x 2½ in)
B: any shape measuring 6 x 5 cm (2¼ x 2 in)
C: 14 x 3 cm (5½ x 1¼ in)

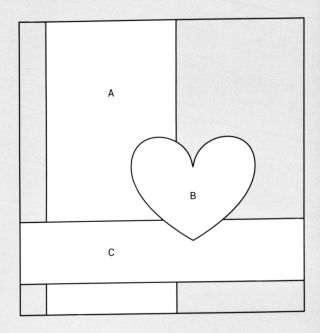

■□□□   MUSIC!

The wide strip on the left-hand side is a combination of cardstock matting and washi tape. The focal point is the treble clef, laser-cut from thin wood.

□■□□   MAGIC MOMENTS

This card can really be made in a jiffy. It is slightly bigger than the template, measuring 15 x 15 cm (6 x 6 in). Both the vertical and horizontal strips are washi tape ribbons. Even the words are simply pasted on.

□□■□   VIBRANT HEART

The stunning patterned paper makes this card special. The bit of coarse raffia, pasted underneath the big heart, finishes the card beautifully. The dashes of glitter glue on the heart and the wide paper strip contribute to the appeal of this striking and flamboyant card.

□□□■   WOODEN FLOWER

The wide vertical strip of pink patterned paper is finished with washi tape. The horizontal paper strip matches the colour scheme perfectly. The wooden flower is a lovely focal point. The tiny wooden blocks ensure a lovely finish.

Square 10

Card: 14 x 28 cm (5½ x 11 in) – fold into a square
A: 12 x 8.5 cm (4¾ x 3⅜ in)
B: circle, 7.5 cm (3 in) in diameter
C: 3 x any shape measuring ± 1 x 1 cm (⅜ x ⅜ in)

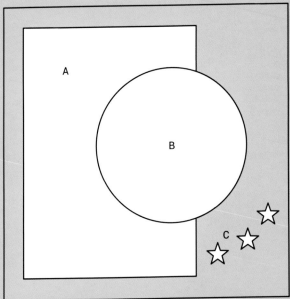

■□□□   HUGGABLE HEDGEHOG

The patterned paper with the letter motif is pasted onto dark-grey paper to highlight pattern. The cute hedgehog is outlined with glitter glue and pasted onto the card with foam tape to add dimension. The picture of the bee is also finished with glitter glue.

□■□□   CLASSY GLAMOUR

The glossy paper used here makes any other embellishment redundant. The small ovals are crystal stickers pasted onto glossy paper, then cut out and pasted onto the card.

□□■□   KITTY-CAT

The card template is followed closely. This is really quick to make because all the components are ready-made stickers. The matting technique used around the cat is very effective and highlights the cat beautifully.

□□□■   WOVEN FOR EFFECT

The large rectangle consists of a woven mat – 1 cm (³⁄₈ in) strips of paper brought together by means of a weaving technique. The strips were cut from three different papers, but six could be even more effective. The mat is placed into a frame of orange card stock and the card finished with a cut out disk over the woven pattern.

Square 11

Card: 14 x 28 cm (5½ x 11 in) – fold into a square
A: 2 half-moons – cut from one circle, 15 cm (6 in) in diameter
B: 14 x 2 cm (5½ x ¾ in)
C: circle, 3 cm (1¼ in) in diameter

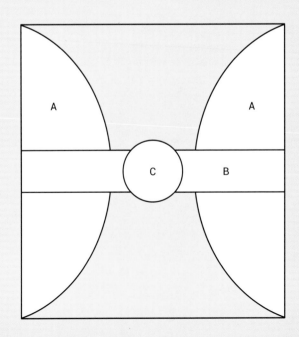

■☐☐☐ **SIMPLE YET STYLISH**

The half-moons on this card have been moved up slightly to maintain the balance since the heart has been adhered lower down on the card face. For a finer finish, a bit of red cord is tied to the fold.

☐■☐☐ **LADYBIRD**

The matting technique used here makes the card extraordinary, and the black, satin-ribbon frame around the edges creates a stunning finish.

☐☐■☐ **EARTHY EASE**

The semi-circles have been replaced by elegant, wavy shapes cut from striking patterned paper. The edges of the paper are chalked to define them. The strip of paper in the centre matches the colour of the card and the patterned paper beautifully. A double-layered flower provides the final touch.

☐☐☐■ **EXCEPTIONAL FLOWER**

The patterned paper used for the semi-circles is stunning. The length of braid and a hessian flower finish this card beautifully.

Square 12

Card: 14 x 28 cm (5½ x 11 in) – fold into a square
Various shapes – copy this more or less
Circles, 1.5 cm (½ in) in diameter

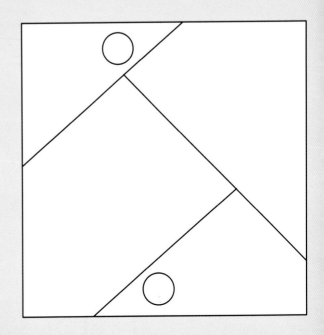

■□□□ SIMPLICITY IN PURPLE AND GREEN

The simplicity is what catches the eye. The colour scheme is very effective, and one corner is left plain so that a message can be added. The various shapes have been cut 0.2 cm (⅛ in) smaller than those indicated on the template to allow the background colour to show, which also highlights the patterned paper.

□■□□ JOLLY PARTY

The vivid, pretty paper strips are neatly finished with ribbon. The colours complement each other. The tiny shoe in the bottom corner is attached with foam tape to add a bit of dimension.

□□■□ ELEGANTLY EMBOSSED

The components are all cut from pearlescent cardstock that is embossed using a Cuttlebug™. The colours go well together and add variation. After all the shapes have been pasted onto the card, grey washi tape is used to provide a neat finish. Two, large self-adhesive rhinestones add the final touch.

□□□■ OLD-WORLD STYLE

The old-world paper used here creates an elegant yet simple card. The edges of the various shapes are finished with a narrow strip of washi tape. Because the paper has such stunning designs, it is not necessary to add the circles indicated on the template.

Square 13

Card: 14 x 28 cm (5½ x 11 in) – fold into a square
A: 3 cm (1¼ in) wide, trim the corners
B: 5 shapes – evenly spaced

■□□□ **HESSIAN FLOWERS**

The diagonal strip is highlighted by the pretty patterned paper used to embellish the triangles on either side of it. The patterned triangles are pasted onto plain cardstock. The diagonal strip is decorated with hessian flowers that complete the card beautifully.

□■□□ **MULTI-COLOURED STARS**

This card is a bit bigger than the template, measuring 15 x 15 cm (6 x 6 in). The emphasis here is on the diagonal strip rather than on the triangles on either side of it. The diagonal strip is made up of two washi tape strips that are pasted right up against each other. Another strip of tape is pasted alongside the wide diagonal strip. The corners are finished with turquoise cardstock that has been embossed using a Cuttlebug™. The matting technique is used to highlight the stars. A pink self-adhesive rhinestones is pasted onto the centre star as the finishing touch.

□□■□ **BLUE BUTTERFLIES**

The various shades of blue with the white of the card are truly striking. Washi tape is pasted on either side of the diagonal strip, and the light and dark-blue butterflies are alternated to finish the card.

□□□■ **BLACK-AND-WHITE**

A fun interpretation of the template makes this combination of black-and-white patterned paper and bows look stunning. Only patterned paper has been used. A white, fabric ribbon with black dots adds a stylish finish.

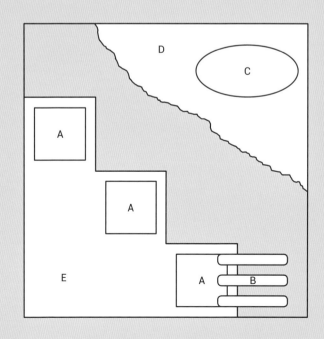

Square 14

Card: 14 x 28 cm (5½ x 11 in) – fold into a square
A: 3 squares, 2.5 x 2.5 cm (1 x 1 in)
B: 3 rectangles, 3.5 x 0.5 cm (1⅜ x ¼ in)
C: oval, 5 x 2.5 cm (2 x 1 in)
D: torn paper to fit the corner of the card
E: shape that accomodates the squares

 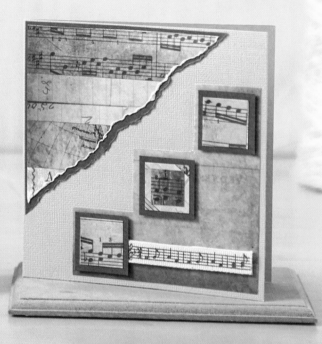

■□□□ WITH LOVE

One length of ribbon has been used instead of the three rectangles. The hearts are pasted onto foam tape to add dimension. The oval is highlighted by the matting technique used to attach it to the card. The ribbon that is pasted over the oval highlights the text and serves as a lovely finish.

□■□□ PIRATE MERRIMENT

This card is very cleverly and interestingly put together. The 'water' is created by the torn paper, and the steps are decorated with pictures that suit the pirate theme. The vivid colours contribute to the finish and match the theme perfectly.

□□■□ USING STRING AND FLOWERS

The squares on the card are cut out, and flowers are pasted onto two of the squares with foam tape. The bits of string are attached using split pins. Stunning patterned paper is used for the torn section. A tiny flower, instead of an oval, finishes this card beautifully.

□□□■ MUSIC A LA CARTE

The torn section is created using a double layer of paper; darker paper is used for the first layer to highlight the patterned paper. The squares are pasted onto the steps, using foam tape to add a little dimension. A single strip of ribbon with a musical note motif serves as the fabulous finish.

Square 15

Card: 14 x 28 cm (5½ x 11 in) – fold into a square
A: 13 x 13 cm (5⅛ x 5⅛ in)
B: 12 x 12 cm (4¾ x 4¾ in)
C: 3 x 3 cm (1¼ x 1¼ in)

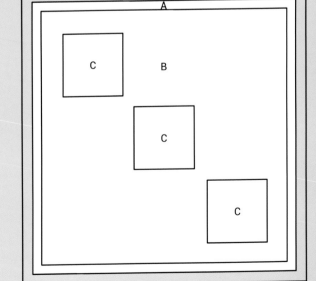

■□□□ PURPLE AND PINK

The squares on the card are small, acrylic tiles. The background is achieved by dripping purple and pink alcohol ink onto the tiles and allowing the colours to blend. When the ink is dry, a flower motif is stamped onto each tile. The squares are pasted onto the card with glue dots. The dark purple edge around the light pink card highlights the purple of acrylic tiles.

□■□□ TRENDY BLACK AND WHITE

The simplicity of this card makes it charming. The floral patterned paper behind the striped paper highlights the plain white flowers pasted on the black squares.

□□■□ EYE-CATCHING TURQUOISE

The outside edges are lined with washi tape, the colour of which matches the punched butterflies in their dark frames beautifully. The square in the centre is finished with a self-adhesive rhinestone. The rhinestones on the butterflies add that final touch.

□□□■ SOFT AND FEMININE

The fact that the three squares are not pasted diagonally in a straight line creates a lovely alternative design. The matting technique is used for all the squares, and they are pasted onto the card with foam tape to add a little dimension.

Square 16

Card: 14 x 28 cm (5½ x 11 in) – fold into a square
A: 13 x 13 cm (5⅛ x 5⅛ in)
B: 5 x 5 cm (2 x 2 in)
C: 11 x 5 cm (4¼ x 2 in)

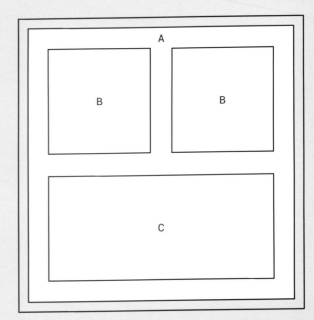

■□□□ BABY BOY

The shades of blue and the blue patterned paper match beautifully. The squares and the rectangle have been lightly sanded with fine sandpaper to achieve a distressed look. The rest of the card is decorated using stickers.

□■□□ FOR DAD

The squares and rectangle on this card are cut out to display the patterned paper on the reverse side of the card face. Metallic shapes are used to embellish the card. It is the ideal Father's Day or birthday card for a man.

□□■□ QUILLED TO PERFECTION

Paper quilling is an ancient art that involves rolling and shaping thin strips of paper. Delicate curls are used to create a variety of three-dimensional objects. Some of my friends are convinced that quilling is addictive. The quilling on this card is highlighted by the bright cardstock frames.

□□□■ PRIMA BALLERINA

Here the rectangle and squares are pasted onto the background. The black and pink create a lovely contrast. The small stickers, attached with foam tape, finish the card beautifully.

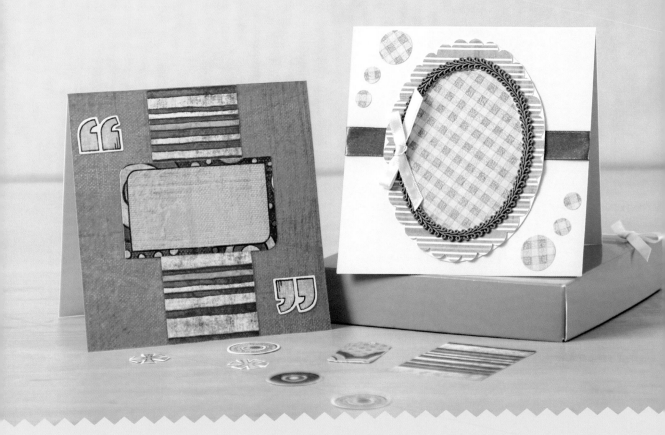

Square 17

Card: 14 x 28 cm (5½ x 11 in) – fold into a square
A: 14 x 3.5 cm (5½ x 1⅜ in)
B: oval, 10 x 9 cm (4 x 3½ in)
C: oval, 5.5 x 4.5 cm (2⅛ x 1¾ in)
D: circle, 1 cm (⅜ in) in diameter

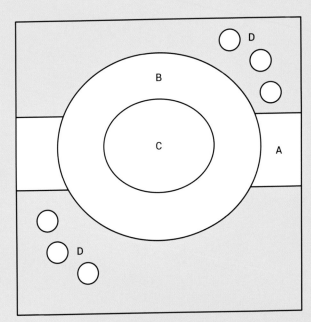

■□□□ **SIMPLY STICKERED**

All the elements on this card are stickers that have simply been pasted onto the background. The colours match perfectly and the card can be made in jiffy.

□■□□ **DELICATE IN BLUE**

The oval is strikingly finished with cord and a bow. The darker blue ribbon underneath the oval highlights the inner edge, and the chequered paper in the centre of the oval complements the striped outer edge perfectly.

□□■□ **ADORABLE GIRAFFE**

A wide, coarse ribbon is contrasted by the giraffe sticker and the jolly orange and blue buttons. The sticker is attached with foam tape, which adds a little dimension and provides a charming finish.

□□□■ **CHIC AND STYLISH**

This card looks very elegant due to the combination of colours. The centre oval of the template is replaced by a rectangle of acetate onto which a motif has been laser-printed. A white milky pen is used to highlight the motif, and a split pin is used on the centre of the flower that is pasted onto the rectangle. The dark-blue ribbon is the finishing touch.

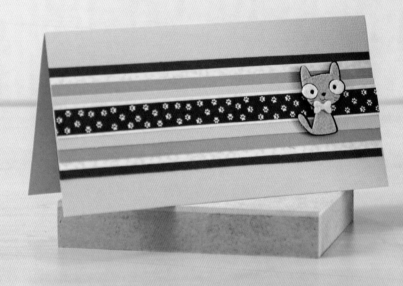

Templates for oblong cards

Oblong 1

Card: 21 x 21 cm (8¼ x 8¼ in)
— fold along length
A: 21 x 0.6 cm (8¼ x ¼ in)
B: 21 x 0.9 cm (8¼ x ⅜ in)
C: 21 x 1.5 cm (8¼ x ½ in)
D: any shape ± 7 x 7 cm (2¾ x 2¾ in)

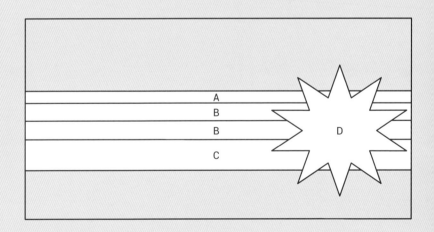

These cards look very elegant. All the templates can be rotated to be used either for a top- or a side-folded card.

■□□□ **CHARMING CAT**

Instead of using single strips of cardstock and paper, the matting technique is used for multi-layering, which lends symmetry to the design. The first layer is black, followed by yellow, blue, light-grey, and a narrower strip of yellow that is covered by an even narrower strip of washi tape. The focal point is a ready-to-use cat shape wearing a bright yellow bow tie, which 'ties' together all the colours beautifully.

□■□□ **STYLISH FLOWER**

A washi tape arrangement in the centre of the card replaces the vertical strips of cardstock or paper. The individual ribbons are approximately 1 cm (3/8 in) wide. The focal point consists of two circles of differ sizes pasted onto each other, with a ready-to-use paper flower adding the finishing touch.

□□■□ **PINK CUPCAKES**

Here, the torn strips of paper in varying widths provide an interesting change to the design. The top strip often overlaps the left edge of the strip onto which it is pasted. Use a special ruler for tearing to ensure that the torn edges look neat. The ready-to-use embellishment in the shape of an iced cupcake is attached using foam tape to add dimension.

□□□■ **LIVE YOUR DREAMS**

Strips A to C have been replaced by strips of washi tape that vary in width. Harmony is achieved by using various patterns in the same colour scheme. The position of the ready-to-use paper flower has been changed to suit its size, and it is balanced perfectly by the message in the form of a sticker. The floral theme is reinforced by the punched flowers.

Oblong 2

Card: 21 x 21 cm (8¼ x 8¼ in)
    – fold along length
A: 20.5 x 10.5 cm (8⅛ x 4¼ in)
B: 2.5 cm x 2.5 cm (1 x 1 in)

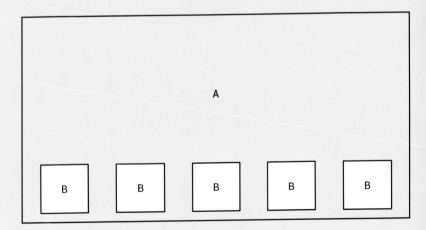

■□□□ CHRISTMAS TREES

Section A consists of red, textured paper, while B is made up of squares; their bases are larger than indicated on the template. The squares consist of various layers of glossy paper that are attached with foam tape to add dimension.

□■□□ FLOWERY CHRISTMAS

A second piece of lovely Christmassy paper is pasted onto section A. The five squares that make up section B have been replaced by punched cardstock flowers, onto which more festive embellishments are pasted to add the finishing touches.

□□■□ COLOURED PEEPHOLES

The matting technique is not used here, and the squares that make up section B are replaced by punched circles around which brightly coloured cardstock circles are pasted as frames. Punched curls in the same colour as the frame are pasted onto the inside of the card so they can be seen through the holes. A multi-coloured, satin cord is knotted in the fold to provide a stunning finish.

□□□■ SQUARE PEEPHOLES

The card is not layered and the squares in section B are punched instead of being pasted onto the card. They are framed to define and finish them. Felt rolls and buttons are pasted onto the inside of the card so that they are visible through the square frames. The thin strip of dark-grey washi tape that is pasted near the fold and the narrower strips of paper used for the frames finish the card beautifully.

Oblong 3

Card: 21 x 21 cm (8¼ x 8¼ in)
– fold along length
A: 20 x 9.5 cm (7¾ x 3¾ in)
B: 18 x 7.5 cm (7⅛ x 3 in)
C: 4.5 x 2.5 cm (1¾ x 1 in)
D: 2.5 x 2.5 cm (1 x 1 in)
E: 7.5 x 1 cm (3 x ⅜ in)
F: 14 x 1 cm (5½ x ⅜ in)

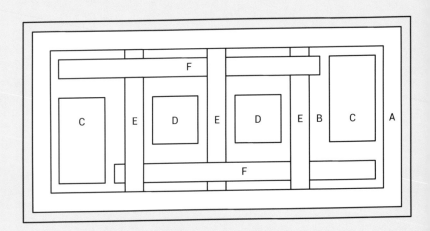

■□□□ BRAID AND CARDSTOCK

The directions for sections A and B are followed exactly. The size of the second rectangle labelled C is adapted to accommodate the text. The strips labelled E and F are lengths of braid. Smaller squares, cut from the same cardstock that is used for the rectangles in section C, are pasted onto the squares in section D to provide a stylish finish. They are attached with foam tape to add dimension.

□■□□ EMBOSSED BLOCKS

Sections A and B are replaced by a washi tape frame. Embossed cardstock is used for sections C and D. The simplicity of the arrangement allows the patterns to stand out beautifully. The narrow ribbons of washi tape used for sections E and F focus the attention on the embossed shapes.

□□■□ SUNFLOWER GREETING

The basic template is followed for sections A and B, while the blocks in sections C and D are embellished with sunflowers and buttons respectively. The patterned paper used for the strips in section F ties all the colours together, and the glossy ribbon used for section E provides a stunning finish.

□□□■ WOODEN SHAPES ON PATTERNED PAPER

Brightly patterned paper is used for both large sections of the design. Section A's purple-and-white dotty paper is contrasted beautifully by the floral paper with a glitter finish used for B. Instead of using the regular strips for E and F, as indicated on the template, washi tape ribbons of varying widths and colours are used to frame sections C and D. Wooden figurines and other ready-to-use embellishments replace C and D.

Oblong 4

Card: 21 x 21 cm (8¼ x 8¼ in)
– fold along length

A: 20 x 9.5 cm (7¾ x 3¾ in)

B: 18 x 7.5 cm (7⅛ x 3 in)

C: 6.5 x 1.5 cm (2½ x ½ in)

D: 4.5 x 1 cm (1¾ x ⅜ in)

E: circle, 1.5 cm (½ in) in diameter

F: 3 x 3 cm (1¼ x 1¼ in)

G: 3 x 1 cm (1¼ x ⅜ in)

H: 1 x 1 cm (⅜ x ⅜ in)

I: 1.5 x 1.5 cm (½ x ½ in)

J: circle, 3 cm (1¼ in) in diameter

K: circle, 0.5 cm (¼ in) in diameter
   (self-adhesive rhinestones
   can also be used)

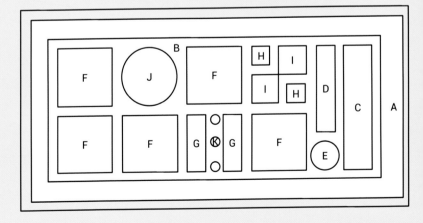

■□□□ EMBOSSED GEOMETRIC SHAPES

Instead of sections A and B, an oblong white frame is used on the grey card face to frame the geometric shapes. The sides are 1 cm (⅜ in) wide. The shapes are cut and punched from cardstock with a glossy finish that has been embossed using various patterns (dies). Instead of using self-adhesive rhinestones for the circles in section K, G is repeated.

□■□□ PASTEL FOR A BABY

A paper frame (with sides measuring 1 cm (⅜ in)) is used around the geometric shapes in the place of sections A and B. A combination of punched shapes, cut paper strips and ready-to-use stickers with a baby theme create the geometric shapes. Soft pink-and-white cord is tied in a bow at the top of the fold for a lovely finishing touch.

□□■□ TEXTURE TOUR

Corrugated cardstock, paper with a snake-skin finish, coarsely woven fabric, and a button with an embossed chequered pattern contribute toward the variety of textures used here. Section A consists of a thin textured piece of cardstock, while B has a smoother finish. The texture tour is maintained by replacing the squares of H and I with leaves.

□□□■ LAYER UPON LAYER

The card is made of textured cardstock and, in addition to sections A and B, another oblong section is added, onto which the geometric shapes are pasted. Circles that vary in size are punched and pasted on top of each other, and buttons are pasted onto some of the layered circles. Clear glass stickers on patterned paper are cut out and used to complement the buttons. All the blocks are double-layered and the top layer is attached with foam tape to add dimension.

Oblong 5

Card: 20 x 18 cm (7¾ x 7⅛ in)
   – fold along length
A: 17 x 9 cm (6¾ x 3½ in)
B: circle, 3 cm (1¼ in) in diameter
   – any other shape can be used
C: circle, 3.5 cm (1⅜ in) in diameter
   – any other shape can be used
D: circle, 2 cm (¾ in) in diameter
   – any other shape can be used

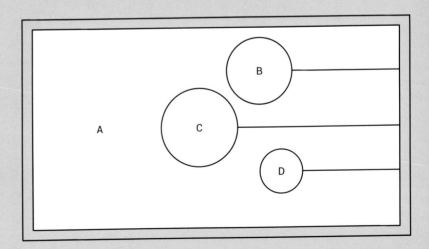

◼☐☐☐ DOVES OF PEACE

The circles have been replaced by doves. The card as well as section A are longer (wider) than indicated on the template to ensure that the shapes do not appear squashed, and to provide enough space for the message. The doves have been cut from embossed paper and finished with silver glitter glue, which is also used for the eyes. Each dove is suspended from a silver cord.

☐◼☐☐ STARRY GLOBES

A wide strip of washi tape with a star motif is pasted against the fold along the full length of the card, replacing section A. Circles and stars in matching sizes are cut from blue and silver patterned paper, punched and layered. A thin strip of silver cardstock replaces the cord.

☐☐◼☐ IRIS-FOLDED CHRISTMAS BALLS

A frame of gold sticky-tape is pasted onto the card face before section A is decorated with iris-folded shapes. Circles in three different sizes are cut into the card face. The iris folding technique is used to create simple balls from thin silver, gold, and purple chocolate foils. These are then pasted onto the matching circles. The balls dangle from gold, silver and multi-coloured cord that are folded over the top of section A before pasted into position.

☐☐☐◼ FESTIVE FLOWERS

Christmassy paper with a glitter finish is used for section A, and a pen is used to draw the cords. Flowers are punched from thin cardstock, and finished with glitter glue and little flower-shaped buttons, before they are attached to the card with thick double-sided tape to add a little height. The raffia bow at the top provides a stunning finish.

Oblong 6

Card: 21 x 21 cm (8¼ x 8¼ in)
– fold along length
A: 21 x 1 cm (8¼ x ⅜ in)
   – ribbon can also be used
B: 2 x 2 cm (¾ x ¾ in)
C: 3 x 3 cm (1¼ x 1¼ in)

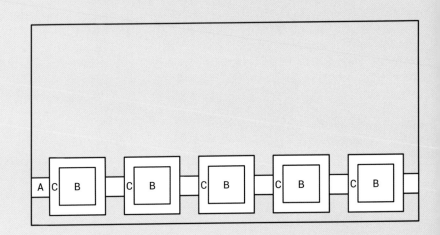

◼☐☐☐ DREAMY FACES

Section A consists of a ribbon of washi tape onto which the squares labelled B and C are pasted. These squares are punched from patterned paper in various colours, and decorated with circles onto which prints resembling old-fashioned photos are pasted matching the theme conveyed by the message. Foam tape is used to attach the photos, thus adding dimension. The message is a printed sticker.

☐◼☐☐ BUTTERFLIES

Washi tape is used for section A; here it has a pink-and-green chevron motif. Matching squares are punched from thin green and pink cardstock and arranged alternately as sections B and C. They provide the double-matted background for the white butterflies that are decorated with self-adhesive rhinestones, and attached using glue dots.

☐☐◼☐ BUDDING CARD

A piece of organza ribbon with silver stripes is used for section A. The squares for C are cut from pink and blue paper with a marble design. Buds mounted on plastic squares replace the squares labelled B. The speckled satin ribbon is tied in a neat bow at the top of the fold for a stunning finish.

☐☐☐◼ GREEN FLOWERS

Speckled washi tape is used for section A. The squares for C are punched from green paper with green specks. Each square is decorated with a creamy-white outer flower and a green inner flower. A cream-coloured button is pasted in the centre. The narrow green cord that is tied in the fold jazzes up the white and keeps the card interesting.

Oblong 7

Card: 21 x 21 cm (8¼ x 8¼ in)
  – fold along length
A: 20 x 1.5 cm (8⅛ x ½ in)
B: 8.5 x 0.5 cm (3¾ x ¼ in)
C: 7.5 x 4.5 cm (3 x 1¾ in)
D: 6.5 x 3.5 cm (2½ x 1⅜ in)
E: circle, 1.5 cm (½ in) in diameter

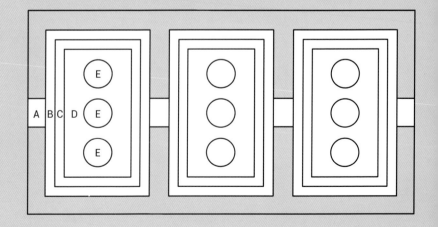

■□□□ **BUTTONS AND RIBBON**

Braid with a square motif and a delicately scalloped edge is used for section A. The template directions are followed for the layered arrangements labelled B, C, and D; these are attached with foam tape to add dimension. The chequered pattern used for section C matches the braid used in A beautifully. Buttons replace the circles in section E.

□■□□ **CHEERFUL FLOWERS**

The bright yellow chevron pattern of the washi tape used for section A is combined with more bright, warm colours in the matted sections with their layers of textured and smooth cardstock. The paper flowers used for the last decorative layer on each matted section are big enough to allow the use of two instead of three. The colours of the cardstock used for the matting are repeated exactly, and self-adhesive rhinestones are used as the centres.

□□■□ **RECTANGLES AND PANES**

Section A consists of a strip of paper with an eye-catching, triangular pattern. The matted arrangements are placed diagonally, and the cardstock rectangles of each arrangement are also turned alternately to create a completely different effect than that indicated by the template. The white punched cardstock squares used for section E are positioned at an angle like panes, and each is decorated with a punched, flowered square which is attached with foam tape to add dimension.

□□□■ **GLOSSY FEMININE FINISH**

Cardstock in soft pastel colours with a strong glossy finish softens the strong lines of the shapes, adding a feminine touch. The scalloped edge of the braid used for section A matches the pastels beautifully, and so do the scalloped edges of the ready-to-use embellishments that are pasted onto the soft lilac labels.

Oblong 8

Card: 21 x 21 cm (8¼ x 8¼ in)
   – fold along length
A: 20 x 9.5 cm (8⅛ x 3¾ in)
B: 13 x 4 cm (5⅛ x 1½ in)
C: 12 x 3 cm (4¾ x 1¼ in)
D: 9 x 7.5 cm (3⅜ x 3 in)
E: circle, 2 cm (¾ in) in diameter
F: split pin
G: ribbon or cord measuring
   ± 35 cm (13¾ in)

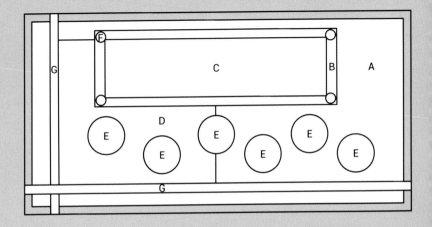

■□□□ THANKS

Patterned paper in various shades of brown is used for the matting, and the same paper is used to punch the background circles for the letters. Sections B and C are not positioned according to the template, and they complement the lettering perfectly. The bottom ribbon is slightly lower than in the template, but it still finishes the card beautifully.

□■□□ FLOWERS AND RIBBON

Soft turquoise and apricot-brown make a stunning colour combination, which is enhanced by the double-layering of sections A and D to match B and C. A decorative wooden flower makes B and C the focal point, while the soft turquoise ribbon ties everything together strikingly. The punched green and apricot flowers with pearl centres are attached with foam tape to add a little dimension.

□□■□ BUTTON BUDDIES

The template is followed almost exactly, with the exception of the added rectangle in the top right-hand side of section A. It ensures that the blue circles, onto which the button arrangement is pasted, stand out clearly. Green and red buttons are used alternately for the button arrangement, and the green, red and blue are repeated in the braid used for G.

□□□■ BALLOON FUN

For this birthday card section D is omitted. The three-dimensional balloon stickers are used instead of the circles in E, with extra stickers pasted onto sections B and C, and where the coloured braid strips cross in the right-hand corner. Four spots of glitter glue replace the split pins in section F, and the message appears in a separate frame created especially for it.

Oblong 9

Card: 21 x 21 cm (8¼ x 8¼ in)
  – fold along length
A: 21 x 1.5 cm (8¼ x ½ in)
B: 7.5 x 2.5 cm (3 x 1 in)

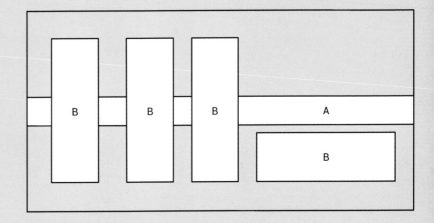

■□□□ HOW DO I LOVE THEE?

The microscope slides used for the rectangles labelled B make this card especially interesting. The vertical rectangles are matted using silver and white cardstock. Paper with a floral pattern is used for the clear slides. The same method is used for the horizontal slide, but the text replaces the floral pattern.

□■□□ FAITH JOY HOPE

The wooden words Faith, Joy and Hope are used instead of the horizontal rectangles indicated on the template. Section A moves to the right-hand edge and the braid is pasted onto double-matted brown and blue cardstock to match the colour scheme. The wooden cross with the carved detail replaces the vertical rectangle, and is mounted beautifully on multi-matted paper with punched, decorative edges.

□□■□ ABSTRACT WITH RHINESTONES

Section A consists of a strip of vellum (satin paper) that is positioned slightly higher than indicated on the template, and decorated with self-adhesive rhinestones. A length of ribbon is pasted close to it. The rectangles labelled B are cut from patterned paper creating abstract motifs in separate blocks. These are double-matted to highlight them. The rhinestone sequence is repeated on the centre rectangle of section B. The fourth rectangle is omitted.

□□□■ FLOWERS GALORE

The template has been followed exactly for this cheerful, orange card. Section A consists of a broad ribbon of washi tape with a busy floral motif. A floral decorative edge is punched along one side of each of the rectangles in section B. The rectangles are pasted onto black cardstock to emphasise the decorative edges. The vertical rectangle is further embellished using dozens of tiny punched flowers.

Oblong 10

Card: 21 x 21 cm (8¼ x 8¼ in)
   – fold along length
A: 20 x 4 cm (7¾ x 1½ in)
B: 3.5 cm x 3.5 cm (1⅜ x 1⅜ in)

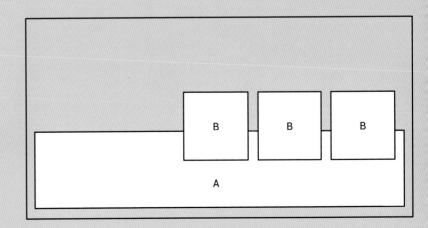

■□□□ POSH GLIMMER

To enhance the pearlescent surface of section A, it is matted on green glitter cardstock and finished using organza ribbon with a silver sheen. The three squares labelled B are matted on the same green glitter cardstock and decorated using little, three-dimensional, silver-and-white flowers.

□■□□ LOVEBIRDS

The same design is given a whole new look here. Broad braid with a lovebird motif is used for section A, and it stands out beautifully against a strip of red washi tape with white stripes. The squares represented by B consist of glossy dark-grey cardstock matted on red. A slight gap is left between the squares and braid strip. The pearls add a stunning finish.

□□■□ BLOCKS AND STRIPES

This card illustrates just how effective the matting technique can be. Section A consists of patterned paper with a block design that is pasted onto plain cardstock that matches one of the pattern colours. The squares labelled B are similarly matted, but foam tape is used to attach them to add a little dimension. Textured paper is used for one of the layers.

□□□■ DOTTY HEARTS

Section A consists of a broad strip of washi tape pasted onto white cardstock to show off its colours. It is then matted on blue cardstock and pasted onto the card. Hearts made up of three layers are used instead of the squares in section B. Orange and blue cardstock are used to punch the bigger hearts, while the smaller ones are punched from the washi tape that is used on the white paper.

Templates for standard-sized cards

Standard 1

Card: half an A4 sheet – fold in half
A: 6.5 x 5.5 cm (2½ x 2⅛ in)
B: 5 x 5 cm (2 x 2 in)
C: hexagon 4.5 x 4 cm (1¾ x 1½ in)
D: 10.5 x 2.5 cm (4½ x 1 in)
E: 3 x pearls or self-adhesive rhinestones

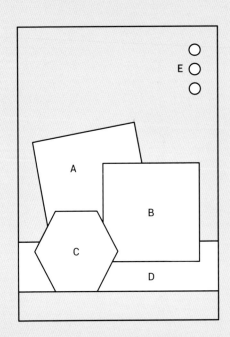

All the standard-sized cards are made using half an A4 sheet of cardstock, so you can make two cards out of one A4 sheet. If you are using bigger pieces of cardstock and cutting them to size, the cut cardstock should measure 30 x 10.5 cm (11¾ x 4¼ in). Each rectangle is then folded in half. These cards will be 0.15 cm (⅛ in) wider than those cut from an A4 sheet.

■□□□ HI!

This jolly card is beautifully finished with glitter glue strips along the edges of the grey square and a few pictures here and there. The word, heart, and little pink bag are attached with foam tape to add dimension.

□■□□ UNFUSSY IN BLACK

This card can be made in a jiffy since you really only have to paste strips of washi tape onto the cardstock. Two squares black-and-white patterns lend an elegant appearance. The bow and three adhesive pearls provide a lovely finish.

□□■□ FROM AN OLD PHOTO ALBUM

The paper used to make the card resembles the photos in a very old album. Foam tape is used to paste the pictures onto various layers of cardstock. The pearls attached to the buttons add a charming finishing touch.

□□□■ BIRD CAGE

All the patterned paper used to make this card matches marvellously. A few strips of washi tape matching the colour scheme have been pasted on both sides of the rectangle. The squares and the circle are emphasised by using the matting technique. The bird cage and self-adhesive rhinestones provide the final finish.

Standard 2

Card: half an A4 sheet – fold in half
A: 12 x 5 cm (4¾ x 2 in)
B: 7.5 x 6 cm (3 x 2¼ in)
C: 14 x 5.5 cm (5½ x 2⅛ in)
D: circle, 3 cm (1¼ in) in diameter
E: ribbon ± 3 cm (1¼ in) long and 1 cm (⅜ in) wide

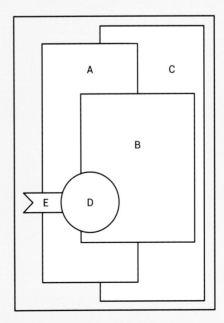

■□□□ ROUND ROSETTE

The template was followed exactly and the interesting combination of colours and patterns makes the card striking. The cream square was embossed beforehand, using a Cuttlebug™ embossing machine. The button on the circle completes the card beautifully.

□■□□ PINK AND PURPLE

The combination of the pink and purple plain and patterned paper works really well on this card. The star and small squares are punched from dark-grey glitter paper and they add some sparkle to the card. The pink organza ribbon provides the finish.

□□■□ SOFTLY FLORAL

The patterned papers go together well. The paper is emphasised by using the matting technique. A corner punch is used to trim the corners of the large square. The card is finished with a punched small pink flower and a tiny white label that is attached to the card with a bit of string.

□□□■ WOODEN FLOWER

The design is adjusted as an extra green strip with one wavy edge has been added. The combination of colours and the large wooden flower make this an interesting card. A small, black paper flower in the centre of the wooden one adds the finishing touch.

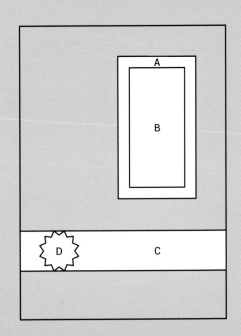

Standard 3

Card: half an A4 sheet – fold in half
A: 7 x 4 cm (2¾ x 1½ in)
B: 6 x 3 cm (2¼ x 1¼ in)
C: 10.5 x 2 cm (4¼ x ¾ in)
D: flower or star

■□□□ **HAT AND BOOT**

The template was followed exactly and the hat and boot form the focal point of the card. The brown strip on the card is spruced up using glitter glue, and the boot and hat are attached with foam tape to add dimension. The combination of colours is very effective.

□□■□ **STRIKING IN BLACK**

Along the bottom, two strips of washi tape are pasted closely together, with only a narrow bit of cardstock visible between them. The focal point, top right, is created by matting polka-dot and black paper. The wooden embellishment matches the colour scheme beautifully and serves as the finish.

□■□□ **JOY!**

This card was made in a few minutes because it is so simple! Despite its simplicity, the colours are really striking and all the elements match beautifully, making this a truly stunning card. Two strips of washi tape are pasted along the bottom – one with a bird motif, and one narrow, black strip. The word sticker complements the card perfectly and gives a lovely finish.

□□□■ **PURPLE BUTTERFLIES**

Purple and pink cardstock strips are pasted onto the left-hand side of the card, using the matting technique, and finished with a ribbon of washi tape. The colours are repeated in the rectangle. The flower and butterfly are laser-cut from thin wood and their colour matches the background perfectly.

86

Standard 4

Card: half an A4 sheet – fold in half

A: 5 x 5 cm (2 x 2 in)

B: 4 x 4 cm (1½ x 1½ in)

C: Torn paper – torn at an angle to fit from corner to corner

D: circle, 3 cm (1¼ in) in diameter

E: circles, 1 cm (⅜ in) in diameter; or use pearls or self-adhesive rhinestones

F: 10.5 x 1 cm (4¼ x ⅜ in)

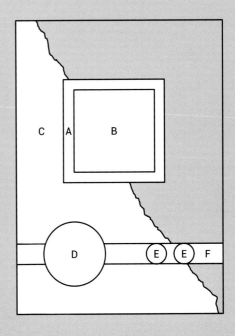

86

◼◻◻◻ ELEGANT IN GREY

The dark-grey patterned paper has been torn neatly using a ruler. The edges are chalked for emphasis. The square is highlighted by pasting smaller squares diagonally onto the larger ones. The smaller squares are punched using a deckle-edge square punch. Washi tape is used for the vertical and horizontal ribbons. The black and white paper flowers provide a stunning finish.

◻◼◻◻ TURQUOISE AND GREY FLOWERS

The template has been adapted slightly and the result is lovely. The blue patterned paper is torn neatly using a ruler, and the edges are chalked. Glue dots are used to attach the blue flowers. A strip of washi tape that matches the colour scheme adds the finishing touch.

◻◻◼◻ GREEN AND ORANGE

The patterned papers match perfectly so no other embellishments are required. The paper is torn neatly using a ruler. The matting technique used to paste the colour-coordinated patterned paper onto the card makes it quite striking. The square and the large circle are attached with foam tape to add dimension.

◻◻◻◼ JUST BECAUSE

The patterned paper and tiny owls in matching colours make this a charming card. The edges of the pink square underneath the big owl are given a glitter-glue lining as a finishing touch. Glitter glue is also used on the patterned paper. The turquoise ribbon with the owl sticker completes the card beautifully.

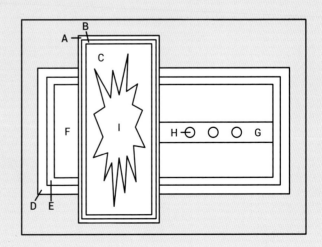

Standard 5

Card: half an A4 sheet – fold in half

A: 9.2 x 4.2 cm (3½ x 1½ in)

B: 8.8 x 3.8 cm (3¼ x 1¼ in)

C: 8.4 x 3.4 cm (3⅛ x 1⅛ in)

D: 12.8 x 6 cm (5⅛ x 2¼ in)

E: 12 x 5.2 cm (4¾ x 2 in)

F: 11 x 4.6 cm (4¼ x 1¼ in)

G: 7 x 1 cm (2¾ x ⅜ in)

H: circles, 0.5 cm (¼ in) in diameter;
   or use pearls or self-adhesive rhinestones

■□□□ **MOTHER AND CHILD**

The focal point of this card is created by the motif stamped on the cardstock. Copper embossing powder is sprinkled over the stamped motif and set using a heat-gun. The horizontal paper strip is embossed using a Cuttlebug™. The matting technique is used for both the vertical and horizontal sections, as indicated on the template. Three squares of wood on the dark-brown centre strip of paper finish the card smartly.

□■□□ **BLUE FLOWERS**

The card can be made quickly because all the elements are simply pasted onto the cardstock. The horizontal strip consists of a wide ribbon of washi tape. The fine flowers, laser-cut from thin wood, are emphasised by the dark-blue cardstock onto which they are pasted. The three, silver-grey pearls provide a lovely finish.

□□■□ **SYMPHONY!**

This work of art is created by combining the right elements. As indicated on the template, the vertical and horizontal strips are attached using the matting technique. The colour combination works exceptionally well. The treble clef mounted in the centre frame of wood not only creates a strong focal point, but also finished this card beautifully.

□□□■ **AFRICAN MASK**

The vivid colours complement the theme of this card well and match the African mask, which is the focal point. Glitter glue is used to highlight the edges of the horizontal orange rectangle, as well as the edges of the vertical gold rectangle. The red and black beads on the strip of gold paper serve as a stunning finishing touch.

Standard 6

Card: half an A4 sheet – fold in half
A: 14 x 1 cm (5½ x ⅜ in)
B: 14 x 9.5 cm (5½ x 3¾ in)
Cut B into various irregular sections.

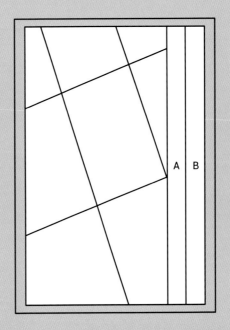

■□□□ TEABAG PATTERN

The template is followed exactly, and the blocks are cut from used teabags that have been dried, cut open and ironed. After attaching the teabags, use a metallic marker to highlight the lines between the bags. The left-hand side of the card is finished using washi tape, and bronze washi tape is also pasted along the edges of the design for a great finish.

□□■□ A TOUCH OF COLOUR

The blocks are cut from various sheets of patterned paper that match marvellously. A touch of colour is included in two of the blocks, which makes the card truly striking. The edges between the blocks are finished using ribbons of thin grey washi tape, while floral washi tape is pasted onto the right-hand side of the card.

□■□□ DRESSED UP

The blocks are cut from an old dress pattern. Ribbon is pasted between the blocks and along the edges of the card. It's finished off with a strip of old-fashioned cream-coloured lace.

□□□■ ROBOTIC FUN

The lovely bright colours of the squares make this an eye-catching design. The edges and the sheen ribbon are finished with glitter glue. The cute robot and gear stickers add the finishing touches.

Standard 7

Card: half an A4 sheet – fold in half
A: 14 x 9.5 cm (5½ x 3¾ in)
B: 13 x 8.5 cm (5⅛ x 3⅜ in)
C: 14 x 1 cm (5½ x ⅜ in) – ribbon can also be used
D: 9.5 x 1 cm (3¾ x ⅜ in) – ribbon can also be used
E: 7 x 5 cm oval (2¾ x 2 in)
F: 8 x 6 cm oval (3¼ x 2¼ in)

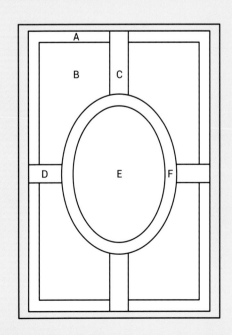

■□□□ FABULOUSLY FASHIONABLE

This is a good example of how a template can be the inspiration for an exceptional card. The layout has been adapted, and the result is very pleasing. The combination of lime-green and black is striking, and the card is finished beautifully with tiny buttons and a delicate rose.

□■□□ ELEGANT AND QUAINT

The old-fashioned paper and the picture in the centre of the oval give this card an old-school yet stylish appearance. The matting technique used highlights the picture on the oval. Ribbon and patterned paper are used as a finish, and these features are emphasised by the plain black paper onto which they are pasted.

□□■□ FESTIVE HOLLY

The template has been adapted slightly and the oval replaced by a rectangle. The rectangle is laser-cut from thin wood. The red paper with the green dots fits the theme beautifully and highlights the red rectangle on the card. Washi tape is used to create the cross, and this adds a charming finishing touch.

□□□■ CHILD'S CHRISTMAS CARD

The cheerful little bird on the polka-dot oval is so cute. The oval and the white rectangle are finished using glitter glue. The glittery motif on the red paper matches the theme well, and the gold sticky-tape cross is the finishing touch.

Standard 8

Card: half an A4 sheet – fold in half
A: 14 x 9.5 cm (5½ x 3¾ in)
B: 14 x 1 cm (5½ x ⅜ in) – ribbon can also be used
C: shapes in 2 different sizes
D: self-adhesive rhinestones or pearls

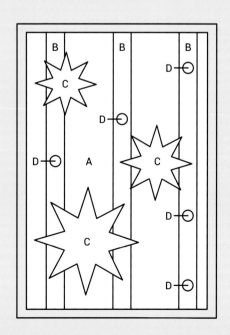

■□□□ **TURQUOISE FLOWER**

The three ribbons on the dark background are strips of washi tape. The card is decorated further by a large, laser-cut wooden butterfly, as well as a smaller wooden one. The finish includes a large paper flower with a smaller flower pasted onto it, and a few self-adhesive rhinestones.

□■□□ **PINK AND BROWN HEARTS**

Brown and pink polka-dot fabric ribbon and washi tape with a bird motif are used. The hearts are attached with foam tape to add dimension. The little circles are made of crystal stickers that are attached to hearts, then cut out and pasted onto the ribbon strips.

□□■□ **PARTY PLEASURE**

Lovely vivid colours are used as the background for this cheerful card. Contrasting blue, purple and pink paper strips are added. Two cute stickers are attached with foam tape and the focal point is a small envelope with sequins. The finishing touches are provided by adding a few sequins and fine beads, and using glitter glue to outline the edges of the paper strips and patterned paper.

□□□■ **FRIENDLY PIRATES**

The embellishments and black cardstock make this a striking card. Three washi tape strips are pasted onto the red background, and cute stickers with a pirate theme provide a fun finish.

Standard 9

Card: half an A4 sheet – fold in half
A: 3 x 3 cm (1¼ x 1¼ in)
B: any shape, ± the same size as A

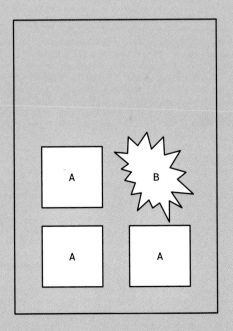

■□□□ HAPPY HUES

Because the design is so simple, the card is simple yet very appealing. The brightly coloured cardstock squares are finished with glitter glue. The pictures of tubes of paint are pasted onto the card with foam tape to add dimension.

□■□□ FROM THE HEART

The paper with a heart motif is pasted onto white cardstock squares to highlight it. The punched white and black hearts provide the finishing touch and, finally, a word sticker to match the theme is added.

□□■□ BUTTERFLY FUN

The paper with a butterfly motif is highlighted by pasting it onto squares of a contrasting colour. The butterflies are punched from the same cardstock as the squares underneath the butterfly paper. The adhesive pearls on the butterflies provide a lovely finish.

□□□■ SOFT AND DELICATE

As the squares on this card have been punched from gorgeous paper, it is not necessary to draw more attention to them. The added rectangle of subtle green paper and the light green lace provide an interesting alternative to the design. The wooden flower with the button centre serves as a lovely finish.

Standard 10

Card: half an A4 sheet – fold in half
A: 2.5 x 2.5 cm (1 x 1 in)
B: Ribbon or washi tape
C: 8 x 2.5 cm (3¼ x 1 in)
D: 7 x 1.5 cm (2¾ x ½ in)
E: 6 x 0.5 cm (2¼ x ¼ in)

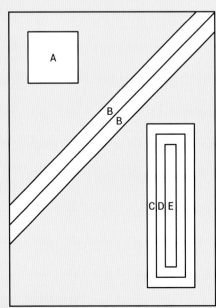

■□□□ WOODEN BUTTERFLY

The diagonal strip consists of cardstock, and the colour contrast is eye-catching. The wooden embellishment is beautifully emphasised by the matting used to attach it to the card. The three adhesive pearls serve as the finish.

□■□□ DOTTED FUN

The diagonal ribbon consists of washi tape strips that are pasted onto the cardstock. A sticker on the left adds text. The white cardstock rectangle on the right highlights the metallic flower beautifully. The polka-dot background is achieved by pasting washi tape onto white cardstock before cutting out the rectangle. The self-adhesive rhinestone in the centre of the flower provides the final touch.

□□■□ WIRE FLOWER

The diagonal strip is achieved by pasting embossed cardstock triangles in the opposite corners of the card. The cardstock triangles are embossed using a Cuttlebug™, and the edges are finished with glitter glue. A strip of gold sticky-tape is pasted underneath the top triangle. The word on the smaller triangle is attached with foam tape and finished with glitter glue. The wire flower is pasted onto glossy cardstock for emphasis. The heart on the flower is finished with glitter glue.

□□□■ TRAVELLING

The two diagonal ribbons consist of strips of washi tape that are first mounted on cardstock and then attached to the card using foam tape. The word sticker is pasted onto turquoise cardstock which, in turn, is pasted onto a light-grey rectangle before it is attached to the card. The finishing touch is the 'stamp' in the right-hand corner. It consists of three cardstock squares in different sizes that are punched and layered before being attached to the card. The top square is attached with foam tape to add dimension.

Standard 11

Card: half an A4 sheet – fold in half
A: 14.8 x 1 cm (6 x ⅜ in)
B and C: any shape in two different sizes
D: self-adhesive rhinestones

■□□□ LARGE FLOWER

The simplicity of this card is what makes it really exceptional. Washi tape is pasted along the bottom and the focal point is the large paper flower with a smaller wooden one attached to it. It creates a lovely finishing touch.

□■□□ HUMBLE HEARTS

The ribbon on the left-hand side of the card is washi tape, and it is beautifully finished with self-adhesive rhinestones. Three hearts of various sizes and colours complete the card.

.

□□■□ QUILLED BUTTERFLY

Even though the design is so simple, the card looks cheerful with its many sequins, pearls, and self-adhesive rhinestones. The butterfly is quilled. The circle and two squares anchor the butterfly and emphasise the quilling as the focal point.

□□□■ SWEETLY FRAMED

The template has been adapted slightly by placing the focal point in the centre of the card. The circle is cut out of white cardstock, and a pretty felt flower is pasted in the centre. A cheerful green ribbon and small buttons provide a charming finish.

Standard 12

Card: half an A4 sheet – fold in half
A: 14 x 9.5 cm (5½ x 3¾ in)
B: 9.5 x 1 cm (3¾ x ⅜ in)
C: 14 x 1 cm (5½ x ⅜ in)
D: round shape, 4.5 cm (1¾ in) in diameter
E: circle, 1.5 cm (½ in) in diameter
F: circle, 1 cm (⅜ in) in diameter
   – self-adhesive rhinestone can also be used
G: self-adhesive rhinestones

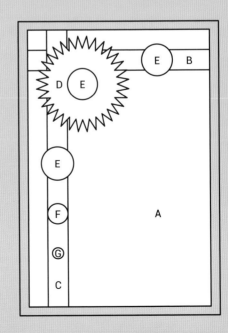

◼◻◻◻◻ CLASSIC LACE

The black lace used here is actually a serviette that is pasted onto a white cardstock rectangle with decoupage glue beforehand. After the decoupage glue has dried completely, the rectangle is attached to the red card. Complementing red washi tape strips are pasted onto the card. The final touches are the large double-layered flower and the smaller ones adorned with black self-adhesive rhinestones.

◻◼◻◻◻ ROCK 'N ROLL

The template can also be rotated and used as a top-folded card. Red washi tape is pasted onto black cardstock strips. The card is decorated with stickers that match the theme. It is a cute card for a teenager.

◻◻◼◻◻ PURPLE SPIRELLI

The 'flower' in the left-hand corner of the card is made with cardstock and embroidery thread, using the spirelli technique. The cardstock edges are notched and the thread is wound around the points to resemble a flower. A large self-adhesive rhinestone provides a stunning finish, echoed by the purple fabric ribbon with rhinestones of various sizes pasted onto it.

◻◻◻◼◻ SUNGLASSES

An interesting variation here is the ribbon that is pasted over the squares. The handbag and sunglasses stickers are pasted over the ribbon. Tiny purple buttons on the ribbon and glitter glue on the handbag and sunglasses add the finishing touches.

◻◻◻◻◼ ORANGE AND PURPLE

The template can be rotated to make this a top-folded card. The card is really simple yet striking because the colours are so extraordinary and match perfectly. Washi tape is used for the ribbons and the rest of the elements are punched shapes in pretty colours that go well together. The cardstock is layered, using foam tape to add dimension.

Standard 13

Card: half an A4 sheet – fold in half
A: 14 x 9.5 cm (5½ x 3¾ in)
B: circle, 3 cm (1¼ in) in diameter
C: circle, 2 cm (¾ in) in diameter
D: circle, 1 cm (⅜ in) in diameter
Paste B – D onto each other

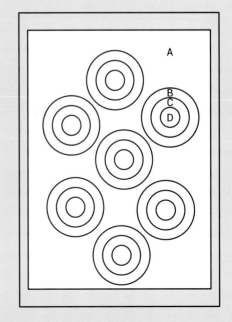

■□□□ **DELICATE ROSES**

The patterned paper is cut to include a rose in each circle. The rose circles are pasted onto the larger circles with foam tape to add dimension. The pastel colours ensure a stunning finish.

□■□□ **FELT AND BUTTONS**

Circles of different sizes and in various colours are cut from felt, and B and C are sewn together with a button in the centre. The circles are pasted onto a white, cardstock rectangle that has been embossed using a Cuttlebug™. Add a lovely finishing touch by bending a brightly coloured pipe cleaner into the shape of three leaves.

□□■□ **CLASSIC FLOWERS**

The cream paper flowers are combined in various ways and pasted onto the cardstock. The centres of the flowers are decorated with adhesive pearls. The decorative wooden card corners provide a stylish finish.

□□□■ **BLOOMING BEAUTIFUL**

The patterned paper with its unique design is really quite something. It forms the base onto which the paper and fabric flowers are arranged and pasted.

Standard 14

Card: half an A4 sheet – fold in half
A: 13 x 1.5 cm (5⅛ x ½ in)
B: 12 x 1.5 cm (4¾ x ½ in)
C: 11 x 1.5 cm (4¼ x ½ in)
D: 9 x 2.5 cm (3½ x 1 in)
E: 8 x 6.5 cm (3¼ x 2½ in)
F: 7 x 5.5 cm (2¾ x 2⅛ in)
G: any shape, ± 4.5 cm (1¾ in) in diameter
H: circle, 5 cm (2 in) in diameter
I: circle, 6 cm (2¼ in) in diameter

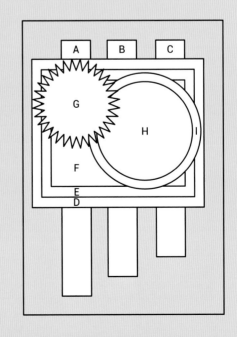

■□□□ **SPIRALS**

The combination of colours used for this card is especially striking and the repetition of the colours is cleverly managed. Washi tape strips are pasted onto the card as the three ribbons. The pretty black, turquoise and pink cardstock is used to layer the rectangle (matting technique). The focal point is the circles and spirals, which immediately catch the eye and contribute to the overall appeal of the card.

□■□□ **HAPPY BIRTHDAY**

The crisp turquoise and white lend a lovely appearance to this card. Turquoise cardstock with various designs is used for the strips and the circle around the message. The message is laser-printed onto acetate or transparency. The focal point is emphasised by the white-and-turquoise paper flower in the corner, and the small pink button on the flower. The stickers on the vertical strips add a lovely final touch.

□□■□ **EARTHY ELEGANCE**

The patterned paper that is used for this card ties everything together beautifully. The edges of the large rectangle and the circles are chalked to give definition and a neat finish. The heart in the corner of the rectangle is made of wood and its edges are also chalked.

□□□■ **CHIC BLACK AND WHITE**

The different combinations of black and white are chic and striking. Three strips of washi tape are pasted onto the card, and the rectangles consist of cardstock and paper with various black-and-white designs. The circle is a custom-made frame. The focal point is achieved by layering black-and-white paper flowers, and pasting a self-adhesive rhinestone in the centre for a lovely finish.

Standard 15

Card: half an A4 sheet – fold in half
A: Diagonal strip 3 cm (1¼ in) wide
B: Diagonal strip 0.5 cm (¼ in) wide
C: 4.5 x 4.5 cm (1¾ x 1¾ in)
D: 1 x 1 cm (⅜ x ⅜ in) – self-adhesive rhinestones
   can also be used

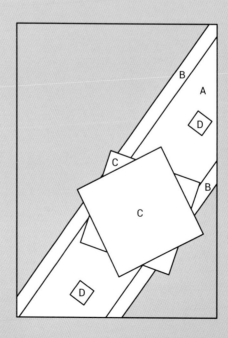

■□□□ TINY FROGS

This card is slightly larger, cut to measure 15 x 12 cm (6 x 4¾ in). The interesting combination of colours makes it striking. The card is very easy to make as all the elements are simply pasted on. The diagonal red cardstock strip is finished by pasting washi tape along both sides. The cardstock squares in the centre are pasted onto the card with foam tape to add a little dimension. Each of the tiny frogs is covered by a square clear sticker before being pasted onto a dark-green background.

□■□□ TEABAG SQUARE

The dimensions are slightly larger, cut to measure 15 x 12 cm (6 x 4¾ in). The diagonal strip is created by pasting triangles of patterned paper in opposite corners of the card. Blue organza ribbon with white dots is pasted along the inside edges of the triangles. The focal point is a design made using the teabag-folding technique. Two square self-adhesive rhinestones add the final touch.

□□■□ WOODEN FLOWER

A diagonal strip of brown cardstock is finished by pasting washi tape along both sides. The focal point is a wooden flower which is emphasised by the lighter shade of the cardstock underneath it. Delicate pink paper flowers with rhinestones in their centres add the finishing touch.

□□□■ PINK HEART

Washi tape is used for the wide diagonal strip. Narrow ribbons of washi tape are pasted along both sides of the wide tape strip. Two purple squares with a punched pink heart form the focal point. White paper flowers with rhinestones in their centres provide a lovely finish.

Standard 16

Card: half an A4 sheet – fold in half
A: Any shape, 3 cm (1¼ in) in diameter

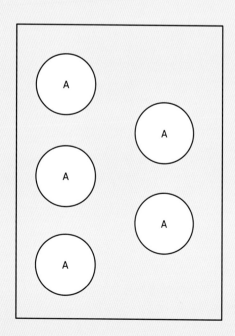

■□□□ CHEERFUL FLOWERS

This is a very simple card, with coloured flowers pasted onto white cardstock. Smaller flowers are pasted in the centre of the cardstock flowers. The cardstock flowers are finished with glitter glue and a piece of fine, peach blow ribbon is used to complete the card.

□■□□ BRILLIANTLY COLOURED SHAPES

The shapes arranged on the circles are freely available from craft stores. Combining various shapes in different sizes makes for an eye-catching card. Self-adhesive rhinestones on all the combined shapes bring the elements together and add sparkle.

□□■□ CHERISH

Ten stars, punched from cardstock in various pastel colours, are pasted onto each other in pairs. A round sticker is pasted onto each star motif. The stars are attached to the card with foam tape to add dimension. The matting technique is used to enhance the word sticker before it is pasted in the corner with foam tape.

□□□■ INTERESTING HEXAGONS

A strip of washi tape is attached to the left-hand side of the card. The pink rectangle deviates slightly from the template, but it finishes the card beautifully. The hexagons are punched in two different sizes.

Standard 17

Card: half an A4 sheet – fold in half
A: Circle, 2.5 cm (1 in) in diameter
B: Wavy rectangle, 5 cm (2 in) wide
C: Wavy rectangle, 5.5 cm (2⅛ in) wide

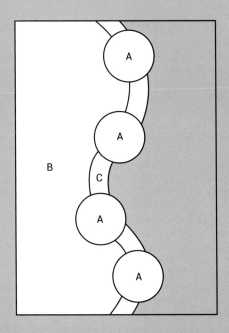

■□□□□ CHRISTMAS ANGELS

The wavy strip in the middle of the card is created by pasting two pieces of patterned paper onto either side of the card. The patterned paper is finished with glitter glue.

□■□□□ TEA PARTY

The template has been adapted slightly – it does not have a double wavy edge. The white paper with rose motif is torn and pasted over a layer of cream and dark-pink paper. A teapot and cups, finished with glitter glue, are cut out and pasted onto the card. A delicate bit of ribbon and a little rose provide the final touch.

□□■□□ CUTE OWLS

This card can be made in a jiffy. The wavy-edged green and grey cardstock is cut using a guillotine. The owls are pasted onto two paper circles of varying sizes before they are attached to the card.

□□□■□ DELICATE BUTTERFLY

The wavy edges have been torn, not cut. The torn edges are chalked and sprinkled with embossing powder, which is set using a heat-gun. A butterfly and little flowers made of hessian are attached to the card with glue dots.

□□□□■ BLUE AND BROWN FLOWERS

A guillotine is used to cut pieces of blue and brown cardstock; the blue must be slightly bigger than the brown. Blue and brown flowers are pasted onto the wavy edge alternately, using glue dots.

Standard 18

Card: half an A4 sheet – fold in half
A: 14.5 x 7 cm (5¾ x 2¾ in)
B: 3 x 3 cm (1¼ x 1¼ in)

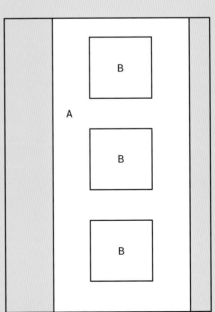

■□□□ METALLIC SHAPES

The squares are cut using a craft knife and finished with patterned paper. Metallic shapes are attached with a thin golden thread that is secured on the reverse side of the little windows with sticky-tape. The thin strips of patterned paper above and below the windows provide a lovely finish.

□■□□ VINTAGE CARS

The pictures of vintage cars are so charming that very little else is needed to make a truly beautiful card. Each car is mounted on dark- and light-brown cardstock, using the matting technique, and then pasted onto the large orange background. A touch of glitter glue on the cars gives the finishing touch.

□□■□ BULKY BUTTONS

A beautiful piece of embossed paper is used for the rectangle on this card. The buttons are mounted on cardstock squares before being pasted onto the card. The edges of the embossed paper are finished with narrow strips of maroon satin ribbon.

□□□■ INTERESTING CIRCLES

The circles on the red background differ slightly, and are punched using a circle punch and glossy cardstock in shades of white and grey. The edge of the card is neatly finished with a paper lace strip on a red background.

Templates for large cards

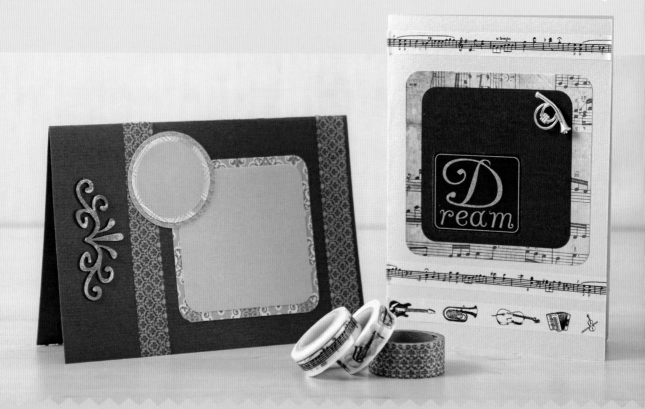

Large 1

Card: A4 sheet – fold along width (A5)

A: 14.5 x 1 cm (5¾ x ⅜ in) – ribbon can be used

B: 12.5 x 11.5 cm (5 x 4½ in) – use a corner punch to trim the corners

C: 10.5 x 9.5 cm (4¼ x 3¾ in) – use a corner punch to trim the corners

D: circle, 5.5 cm (2⅛ in) in diameter

E: 12.5 x 3 cm (5 x 1¼ in) – use a corner punch to trim the corners

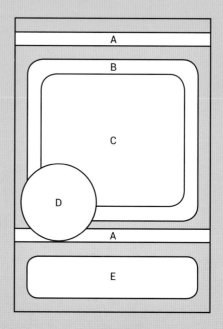

Sometimes one needs to go big! And when the opportunity presents itself, a lovely large card is exactly what you need. Cardstock is generally available in A4 sheets. You simply fold the sheet in half to make an A5-size card.

■□□□ MODEST GREEN

A wide strip of washi tape is used for A.The paper with glitter the finish used for B is repeated in the matt centre circle labelled D to add a bit of sheen. The corners of B and C are trimmed using a punch. The beermat embellishment used for E is chalked to match the background colour.

□■□□ MUSICAL DREAM

One of the greatest joys of cardmaking is the availability of loads of materials that match specific themes. Here, music is obviously the theme, and the paper used for B, as well as the washi tape used for sections A and E, ties in beautifully. Section D conveys the message in the form of a sticker, and the small musical instrument is added as the finishing touch.

□□■□ CAR WITH FLOWERS

The focal point on section C, which is the car, is carefully layered, using several copies of the same picture to create a three-dimensional effect. This calls for precise cutting and accurate pasting of the layers, using foam tape. Outlining with glitter glue adds a bit of sparkle. Note that section D is made up of various elements, yet it does not appear overstated.

□□□■ NEON RECOLLECTIONS

Neon colours will always make an impact. Section C is decorated using the iris folding technique in neon colours. The colours are repeated in the smaller punched flowers pasted into the corners. Components A consist of yellow washi tape ribbons. The cutting technique used in the message block highlights the lettering.

Large 2

Card: A4 sheet – fold along width (A5)
A: 21 x 1 cm (8¼ x ⅜ in) – ribbon can be used
B: 14 x 1 cm (5½ x ⅜ in) – ribbon can be used
C: any shape, measuring ± 6 x 6 cm (2¼ x 2¼ in)

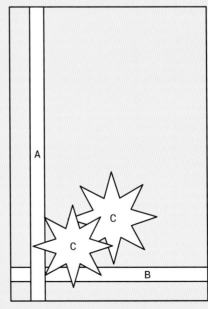

■□□□ DOWN TO EARTH

Given all the interesting embellishments and decorative elements for sale these days, one can really make a stunning card no time. Here, two washi tape ribbons with a simple flower-and-leaf motif are used for sections A and B, and a ready-to-use butterfly and hessian flowers are pasted in position C. It cannot be easier than this!

□■□□ WOODEN HEART WITH FLOWERS

A rectangle of patterned paper covers the largest part of the card and provides a striking background for the wooden heart with decorative detail. Narrow satin ribbon is used for elements A and B. Paper flowers and a satin bow in the wooden heart add a stunning finish.

□□■□ FELT FLOWERS

The bright colours of the felt flowers and the braid are especially striking on the black background. For components C, two double-layered felt flowers are cut and finished using buttonhole stitching in contrasting embroidery thread. The centres are double-layered buttons that are stitched on using embroidery thread.

□□□■ BON VOYAGE

Components A and B consist of strips of polka-dot paper and washi tape; the tape is pasted onto white paper first, so as not to be transparent, and then onto the polka-dot strips. C consists of two circles – each is matted with three layers of matching patterned paper before the message and ready-to-use aeroplane shape are attached. The aeroplane is coloured black using a felt-tip pen, and the beermat lettering is chalked to add a dash of colour.

Large 3

Card: A4 sheet – fold along width (A5)
A: 11.5 x 8.5 cm (4½ x 3⅜ in)
B: 12 x 9 cm (4¾ x 3½ in)
C: 12.5 x 9.5 cm (5 x 3¾ in)
D: 8.5 x 8.5 cm (3⅜ x 3⅜ in)
E: 6.5 x 6.5 cm (2½ x 2½ in)
F: 14.5 x 0.5 cm (5¾ x ¼ in) – ribbon or lace can also be used
G: split pins

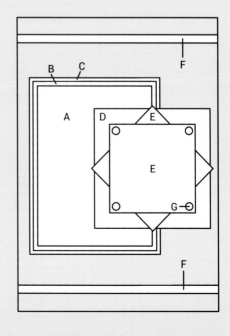

◼☐☐☐ **BLUE AND WHITE**

The various shades of blue look fresh and cheerful on the snow-white background. Using repetition and alternating the two matted sections contribute to the harmony and appeal of the design, while the embossed cardstock adds texture. The white stitch detail on the braid also adds to the overall charm of the card.

☐◼☐☐ **GOLD AND SILVER**

Double-sided scrapbooking paper with various designs can be used effectively to alternate patterns while maintaining the basic colour scheme. Here, the front and reverse sides of such sheets of paper are alternated between the matted components and section F of the template. What really ties everything together beautifully is using layers of gold and silver glitter paper for the matting. The wooden sleigh adds an interesting finishing touch.

☐☐◼☐ **BAGS ARE PACKED**

The brown satin ribbon with stitch detail used for section F provides beautiful border lines. Stickers with a travelling theme and the matting technique used for the cardstock and paper convey the message beautifully. The glossy finish of the stickers is repeated by outlining the edges of section E, while section D is attached with foam tape to add dimension.

☐☐☐◼ **IN THE MOOD FOR LOVE**

Little clouds, hearts and the coloured cardstock birdie contribute to the theme of love. Washi tape, pasted onto light-pink cardstock which, in turn, is pasted onto slightly wider strips of grey cardstock, is used for section F. The matting technique is used for all the squares, and their corners are trimmed with a corner punch. Additional embellishments are pasted onto the bits of imitation wood to create a sense of harmony. The beads are attached using glue dots.

Large 4

Card: A4 sheet – fold along width (A5)
A: 12 x 2 cm (4¾ x ¾ in)
B: circle, 12 cm (4¾ in) in diameter
C: 8.5 x 8.5 cm (3⅜ in)
D: circle, 1 cm (⅜ in) in diameter

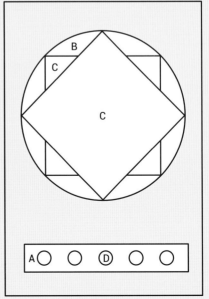

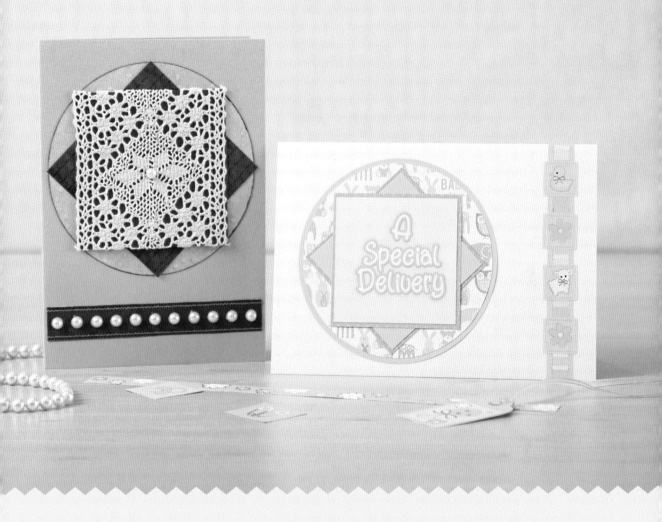

■□□□ GINGERBREAD HOUSE

The silver glitter paper and glossy red cardstock form a striking contrast; the combination is reversed for sections A and B. The gingerbread house used to decorate section C is created three-dimensionally by skilfully cutting and pasting various layers of the same picture. The pearls on the flowers of section A provide a stunning finish, matching the rest of the gloss and glimmer brilliantly.

□■□□ A DASH OF RED

The combination of red, white and black elements is appropriate for both Christmas and Valentine's Day. Embellishments such as hearts and flowers would be more appropriate for Valentine's Day, while Christmas trees and such would better suit the festive season. Here, the elements are fairly neutral, making the card ideal for any occasion.

□□■□ PEARLS AND LACE

Here, section C consists of a square of rusty-brown cardstock, neatly covered with lace that is attached on the reverse side before the square is pasted onto the card. The muted pink circle used for section B is chalked to make it stand out. Section A consists of a cardstock strip with a stitch pattern and it is finished neatly with adhesive pearls.

□□□■ A SPECIAL DELIVERY

The vast variety of materials available makes it very easy to create a personalised card when you wish to congratulate the parents of a new-born. Sections B and C consist of soft pastel colours that are combined using the matting technique, and the repetition results in a sense of harmony. The rest of the embellishments and the message are ready-to-use stickers that match the theme. They are usually available in sets of blue and pink.

Large 5

Card: A4 sheet – fold along width (A5)
A: 13 x 10 cm (5⅛ x 4 in)
B: 10 x 9.5 cm (4 x 3¾ in)
C: circle, 8.5 cm (3⅜ in) in diameter
D: 14.5 x 1 cm (5¾ x ⅜ in) – ribbon can also be used
E: 14.5 x 4 cm (5¾ x 1½ in)
F: self-adhesive rhinestones

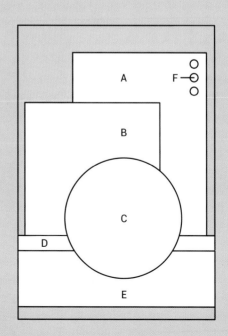

■□□□ SOFT GREEN AND APRICOT

Washi tape is available in hundreds of designs and colour combinations. It can be used as the point of departure when you choose colour combinations, as was the case here, when a strip of tape was used for section D. Because the cream, soft green and apricot look so lovely together, the rest of the paper and embellishments were selected accordingly. Plain windows with rounded corners, cut using a special tool, are used for section C, while coral-coloured buttons are used to highlight section F.

□■□□ EARTHY ABUNDANCE

Various sheets of patterned paper with the same colour scheme are combined to create the elements of the design. The edges of some of the elements that are cut from lighter patterned paper are chalked for emphasis. The striped paper used for section E blends in beautifully with section D.

□□■□ FLORAL FANCY

Grey, green, black and cream create an extraordinary yet striking combination of colours. For section E, the bottom edge of a strip of black cardstock has been punched using a decorative edge punch. Section D consists of a strip of dotty washi tape; B is a cut out of embossed cardstock; and A consists of a thick chunk of patterned paper. The floral combination immediately attracts attention. The rhinestone in the centre of the flower is repeated in the rhinestones pasted onto section F.

□□□■ DOTS AND CIRCLES

A black-and-white combination always looks sophisticated and, thanks to the classic colours, any motif can be used with it. Here various forms of dots and circles have been combined. The individual elements are united by the ribbon of black washi tape used in section D.

Large 6

Card: 26.6 cm x 21 cm (10½ x 8¼ in)
    – fold at 12 cm (4¾ in) along the length
A: 19 x 10.5 cm (7½ x 4¼ in)
B: 18 x 9.5 cm (7⅛ x 3¾ in)
C: 17 x 8.5 cm (6¾ x 3⅜ in)
D: 16 x 7.5 cm (6¼ x 3 in)
E: 12 x 3 cm (4¾ x 1¼ in)

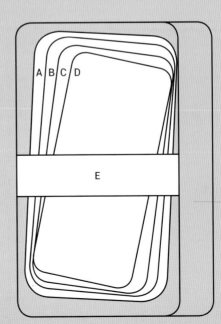

■□□□ LILAC AND RIBBON

The card has a protruding strip that can be used either for embellishments or the message. Patterned paper and embossed cardstock in various shades of lilac are used for the layered card face. All the corners are trimmed using a corner punch. The organza ribbon is attached to the card using a split pin to prevent it from slipping off when the bow is untied.

□■□□ CHEERS!

The various layers on the card face are not pasted at an angle; each layer is pasted in the centre of the previous one. An additional layer of embossed blue cardstock is pasted onto the white card front. Section E consists of a vellum (satin paper) strip that is also pasted onto the protruding strip before the bead embellishment is pasted onto it. Three-dimensional wine glass stickers add the finishing touch.

□□■□ BUTTONED-UP

Here the corners are not trimmed, and the layers are not tilted, but left-aligned instead. The layers of patterned paper with a glitter finish and glossy cardstock are alternated with ordinary matt patterned paper and plain dark-green paper. The glossy cardstock used as the base is repeated in the intricate punched design that decorates the protruding strip. The button through which the pearl cord is threaded provides a stunning finish.

□□□■ BE THAT PERSON

The template is followed closely, but the corners are decoratively trimmed instead of rounded. The patterned paper complements the pink background with its glossy finish beautifully, and the protruding strip is decorated with washi tape. The message is placed on the patterned paper section.

Author's acknowledgements

There are so many people who supported me during this project, I am almost at a loss for words. Making more than two-hundred cards is definitely not child's play. Fortunately, my friends were eager to help out and offered their interpretations of the card templates in the most inventive ways! Their creativity never ceased to amaze me, and I learnt so much from each and every one of them. Thank you so much Ilse, Juanelle, Suzaan, Wilsia, Christine, René, Emma, Karen, Madelein, Elna, Corlé and Francia for the stunning cards you made. Ilse, thanks for practically 'moving in' for almost the entire duration of the school break and making sure that I kept on working.

Wilsia, thank you so very much for your help with the descriptions of the cards, and for your patience with me when I was distracted.

Kenny, thanks for always being so professional during the photo sessions. Liezl, thank you very much for the beautiful design that you have come up with yet again, especially since you were under pressure to finish it in such a short time.

I would like to thank my family for their patience. A big thank you to Paul, who was always ready to serve coffee and refreshments during the photo sessions. And to Corlé and Francia, who took turns preparing supper when they realised I was too busy.